TEACHER'S PET PUBLICATIONS

PUZZLE PACK
for
A Farewell to Manzanar

based on the book by
Jeanne Wakatsuki Houston & James D. Houston

Written by
William T. Collins

© 2005 Teacher's Pet Publications
All Rights Reserved

The materials in this packet are copyrighted
by Teacher's Pet Publications, Inc.

These pages may be duplicated by the purchaser
for use in the purchaser's own classroom.

Copying any of these materials and distributing them
for any other purpose is a violation of the copyright laws.

© 2005 Teacher's Pet Publications, Inc.
www.tpet.com

INTRODUCTION
If you already own the LitPlan for this title, this Puzzle Pack will refresh your Unit Resource Materials and Vocabulary Resource Materials sections plus give you additional materials you can substitute into the tests. If you do not already have a complete LitPlan, these pages will give you some supplemental materials to use with your own plan. There are two main groups of materials: one set for unit words (such as characters' names, symbols, places, etc.) and one set for vocabulary words associated with the book.

WORD LIST
There is a word list for both the unit words and the vocabulary words. These lists show you which words are being used in the materials and the clues or definitions being used for those words. You may want to give students a word list with clues/definitions to help them, or you may want students to only have a word list (without clues/definitions) if you want them to work a little harder. Both are available for duplication. The word lists can also be your "calling key" for the bingo games.

FILL IN THE BLANK AND MATCHING
There are 4 each of the fill in the blank and matching worksheets for both the unit and vocabulary words. These pages can be used either as extra worksheets for students or as objective parts of a unit test. They can be done individually if students need extra help or as a whole class activity to review the material covered.

MAGIC SQUARES
The magic squares not only reinforce the material covered but also work on reasoning and math skills. Many teachers have told us that their students really enjoy doing these!

WORD SEARCH PUZZLES
The word search words go in all directions, as indicated on your answer keys. Two of the word search puzzles have the clues listed rather than the words. This makes the puzzle a little more difficult, but it reinforces the material better. Two word search puzzles have words only for students who find the clue puzzles too difficult.

CROSSWORD PUZZLES
Both unit and vocabulary word sections have 4 crossword puzzles.

BINGO CARDS
There are 32 individual bingo cards for the unit words and 32 individual bingo cards for the vocabulary words. You can use your word list as a "call list," calling the words at random and marking them off of your list as you go, or you could use the flash cards by cutting them apart and drawing the words at random from a hat (or box or whatever). To make a better review, you might ask for the definition and spelling of each word as you call it out–or you could call out the definitions and have students tell you the words they need to look for on the puzzle.

JUGGLE LETTERS
The vocabulary juggle letter game is intended to help students learn the spellings of the words. One sheet has the definitions listed on it as an extra help for students who need it or to reinforce the definitions if you choose to do so.

FLASH CARDS
We've included a set of vocabulary flash cards you can duplicate, cut, and fold for your students. Some teachers make a few sets for general use by the class; others make a set for each student. Some teachers duplicate them for each student and have the students cut & fold their own. You can cut out just the words and put them in a hat, have each student pick out one word and write the definition and a sentence for that word. Students then swap words and papers, with the next student adding a sentence of his own under the last one. You can have students swap as many times as you like. Each time the student will read the sentences written prior to his own and then add a sentence. You can cut out the words and definitions separately and play "I Have; Who Has?" Each student in the room draws a word and definition. The first student says, "I have (the name of the word). Who has the definition?" The student with the definition reads it then says, "I have (the name of the vocabulary word she has). Who has the definition?" The round continues until all words and definitions have been given.

Farewell to Manzanar Unit Word List

No.	Word	Clue/Definition
1.	ATTACK	December 7, 1941 was the date of the Japanese _____ on Pearl Harbor
2.	BALLET	Jeanne thought it was a misuse of the body
3.	BARRACKS	Block 16 was the location of the first _____ the family lived in
4.	BILL	Jeanne's older brother; led a dance-band; sent to Germany
5.	BUDDHIST	Family's religion
6.	CABRILLO	_____ Homes; where the family lived after the war was over
7.	CANE	Papa's version of the samurai sword
8.	CATHOLIC	Religion to which Jeanne wanted to convert
9.	CHIZU	Woody's wife
10.	CITIZENS	Public Law 414 allowed Japanese-Americans to become US _____
11.	CLOSED	December 5, 1945 Manzanar camp officially _____
12.	COMBAT	442nd _____ Regiment was an all Nisei unit in the US Army
13.	CONGRESS	In 1924 immigration from Japan was stopped by US _____
14.	COOPERATIVE	Papa drafted plans to start one but never started it
15.	DIETICIAN	Mama's job at the camp
16.	DISLOYALTY	Greatest possible disgrace for a Japanese man to be charged with
17.	ELEANOR	Jeanne's older sister; re-entered camp; had a baby in camp
18.	ELEVEN	Age of Jeanne's daughter when they went to the camp
19.	EMIGRATION	In 1886 the Japanese government lifted its ban on _____
20.	ENDO	Mitsue ___ protested internment under habeas corpus & won
21.	ENGLISH	Language Jeanne spoke
22.	EVACUATION	Hirabayashi & Korematsu challenged racial bias of _____ order & lost
23.	EXCLUDE	Executive Order 9066 allowed the military to _____ people from Western areas
24.	FAMILY	Mess hall caused the disintegration of the _____
25.	FISH	Mama worked at the ___ cannery
26.	FISHERMAN	Papa's job before internment
27.	FRED	Mr. Tayama's first name; he was beaten at camp and almost died
28.	HARBOR	Pearl ___; American base in Hawaii bombed by Japan
29.	HIROSHIMA	August 6, 1945 US dropped atom bomb on _____
30.	IMMIGRANTS	In 1869 the first Japanese _____ arrived in the US
31.	INLAND	August 12, 1942 Evacuation to ten _____ camps was completed
32.	INTERVIEWER	Papa's job at Ft. Lincoln
33.	INU	Traitor; women called Papa this
34.	JAPAN	Ka-Ke; Papa's home in _____
35.	JERSEY	Several of Jeanne's family members moved to New ___ after the war
36.	JOE	Mr. Kurihara; leader of Manzanar camp riot
37.	JOSE	San _____; family home for Jeanne's last year in high school
38.	KAZ	Foreman of the reservoir crew
39.	KIYO	Jeanne's brother; punched Papa in the face to protect Mama
40.	KO	Papa's first name
41.	LINCOLN	Ft. _____; Papa was imprisoned there
42.	LOYALTY	Oath Japanese-American men were asked to sign
43.	MANZANAR	Resettlement camp for Japanese Americans
44.	NASH	Model of car Papa drove out of Manzanar
45.	NINE	Number of months Papa spent at Ft. Lincoln
46.	OCEAN	_____ Park; where Wakatsuki family lived before their internment
47.	ORCHARD	Spring of 1943 the family moved near the peach _____
48.	OWENS	_____ Valley, CA; location of Manzanar camp
49.	QUEEN	Jeanne's elected position; Carnival _____

Farewell to Manzanar Unit Word List

No.	Word	Clue/Definition
50.	RADINE	Jeanne's friend in junior high but not high school
51.	SACRAMENTO	California city where first Japanese immigrants settled
52.	SCOUTS	Girl ___ did not accept Jeanne as a member
53.	SEVEN	Jeanne's age when the family went to Manzanar
54.	SHIG	Eleanor's husband; drafted into US Army
55.	STRAWBERRIES	In 1952 the family moved to San Jose and Papa raised _____
56.	SURRENDER	August 14, 1945 Japan _____ed; WWII ended
57.	TERMINAL	Long Beach was the location of _____ Island
58.	THIRTY	Number of years it took Jeanne to go back to Manzanar
59.	THOUSAND	Number of interned Japanese-Americans: 110 _____
60.	TOMI	Bill's wife
61.	WOODY	Jeanne's older brother; drafted into the US Army; visited Japan

Farewell to Manzanar Fill In The Blank 1

_____ 1. Long Beach was the location of _____ Island

_____ 2. Foreman of the reservoir crew

_____ 3. Executive Order 9066 allowed the military to _____ people from Western areas

_____ 4. San _____; family home for Jeanne's last year in high school

_____ 5. Jeanne's older brother; led a dance-band; sent to Germany

_____ 6. Mama's job at the camp

_____ 7. Block 16 was the location of the first ____ the family lived in

_____ 8. Jeanne's elected position; Carnival _____

_____ 9. Mitsue ___ protested internment under habeas corpus & won

_____ 10. Ft. _____; Papa was imprisoned there

_____ 11. Public Law 414 allowed Japanese-Americans to become US _____

_____ 12. Number of interned Japanese-Americans: 110 _____

_____ 13. Age of Jeanne's daughter when they went to the camp

_____ 14. Several of Jeanne's family members moved to New ___ after the war

_____ 15. Number of months Papa spent at Ft. Lincoln

_____ 16. Spring of 1943 the family moved near the peach ____

_____ 17. California city where first Japanese immigrants settled

_____ 18. In 1869 the first Japanese ____ arrived in the US

_____ 19. Papa's first name

_____ 20. Pearl ___; American base in Hawaii bombed by Japan

Farewell to Manzanar Fill In The Blank 1 Answer Key

TERMINAL	1. Long Beach was the location of _____ Island
KAZ	2. Foreman of the reservoir crew
EXCLUDE	3. Executive Order 9066 allowed the military to _____ people from Western areas
JOSE	4. San ____; family home for Jeanne's last year in high school
BILL	5. Jeanne's older brother; led a dance-band; sent to Germany
DIETICIAN	6. Mama's job at the camp
BARRACKS	7. Block 16 was the location of the first ____ the family lived in
QUEEN	8. Jeanne's elected position; Carnival _____
ENDO	9. Mitsue ___ protested internment under habeas corpus & won
LINCOLN	10. Ft. ____; Papa was imprisoned there
CITIZENS	11. Public Law 414 allowed Japanese-Americans to become US _____
THOUSAND	12. Number of interned Japanese-Americans: 110 _____
ELEVEN	13. Age of Jeanne's daughter when they went to the camp
JERSEY	14. Several of Jeanne's family members moved to New ___ after the war
NINE	15. Number of months Papa spent at Ft. Lincoln
ORCHARD	16. Spring of 1943 the family moved near the peach ____
SACRAMENTO	17. California city where first Japanese immigrants settled
IMMIGRANTS	18. In 1869 the first Japanese ____ arrived in the US
KO	19. Papa's first name
HARBOR	20. Pearl ___; American base in Hawaii bombed by Japan

Copyrighted

Farewell to Manzanar Fill In The Blank 2

_____ 1. Mitsue ___ protested internment under habeas corpus & won

_____ 2. Papa's first name

_____ 3. Eleanor's husband; drafted into US Army

_____ 4. August 12, 1942 Evacuation to ten ____ camps was completed

_____ 5. Mess hall caused the disintegration of the _____

_____ 6. Jeanne's older sister; re-entered camp; had a baby in camp

_____ 7. Spring of 1943 the family moved near the peach ____

_____ 8. ____ Homes; where the family lived after the war was over

_____ 9. Mama worked at the ___ cannery

_____ 10. Model of car Papa drove out of Manzanar

_____ 11. Ka-Ke; Papa's home in _____

_____ 12. Number of years it took Jeanne to go back to Manzanar

_____ 13. Traitor; women called Papa this

_____ 14. Jeanne's age when the family went to Manzanar

_____ 15. Long Beach was the location of _____ Island

_____ 16. Family's religion

_____ 17. ____ Valley, CA; location of Manzanar camp

_____ 18. Jeanne's friend in junior high but not high school

_____ 19. In 1886 the Japanese government lifted its ban on _____

_____ 20. Several of Jeanne's family members moved to New ___ after the war

Copyrighted

Farewell to Manzanar Fill In The Blank 2 Answer Key

ENDO	1. Mitsue ____ protested internment under habeas corpus & won
KO	2. Papa's first name
SHIG	3. Eleanor's husband; drafted into US Army
INLAND	4. August 12, 1942 Evacuation to ten ____ camps was completed
FAMILY	5. Mess hall caused the disintegration of the ____
ELEANOR	6. Jeanne's older sister; re-entered camp; had a baby in camp
ORCHARD	7. Spring of 1943 the family moved near the peach ____
CABRILLO	8. ____ Homes; where the family lived after the war was over
FISH	9. Mama worked at the ____ cannery
NASH	10. Model of car Papa drove out of Manzanar
JAPAN	11. Ka-Ke; Papa's home in ____
THIRTY	12. Number of years it took Jeanne to go back to Manzanar
INU	13. Traitor; women called Papa this
SEVEN	14. Jeanne's age when the family went to Manzanar
TERMINAL	15. Long Beach was the location of ____ Island
BUDDHIST	16. Family's religion
OWENS	17. ____ Valley, CA; location of Manzanar camp
RADINE	18. Jeanne's friend in junior high but not high school
EMIGRATION	19. In 1886 the Japanese government lifted its ban on ____
JERSEY	20. Several of Jeanne's family members moved to New ____ after the war

Farewell to Manzanar Fill In The Blank 3

_____

1. August 12, 1942 Evacuation to ten ____ camps was completed
2. Number of years it took Jeanne to go back to Manzanar
3. Public Law 414 allowed Japanese-Americans to become US _____
4. In 1952 the family moved to San Jose and Papa raised _____
5. Ka-Ke; Papa's home in _____
6. Executive Order 9066 allowed the military to _____ people from Western areas
7. December 7, 1941 was the date of the Japanese _____ on Pearl Harbor
8. Foreman of the reservoir crew
9. Mitsue ___ protested internment under habeas corpus & won
10. Mama worked at the ___ cannery
11. Age of Jeanne's daughter when they went to the camp
12. Mama's job at the camp
13. In 1924 immigration from Japan was stopped by US _____
14. Greatest possible disgrace for a Japanese man to be charged with
15. Spring of 1943 the family moved near the peach ____
16. December 5, 1945 Manzanar camp officially _____
17. Papa's first name
18. ____ Valley, CA; location of Manzanar camp
19. Jeanne's older brother; drafted into the US Army; visited Japan
20. Family's religion

Farewell to Manzanar Fill In The Blank 3 Answer Key

INLAND	1. August 12, 1942 Evacuation to ten ____ camps was completed
THIRTY	2. Number of years it took Jeanne to go back to Manzanar
CITIZENS	3. Public Law 414 allowed Japanese-Americans to become US ____
STRAWBERRIES	4. In 1952 the family moved to San Jose and Papa raised ____
JAPAN	5. Ka-Ke; Papa's home in ____
EXCLUDE	6. Executive Order 9066 allowed the military to ____ people from Western areas
ATTACK	7. December 7, 1941 was the date of the Japanese ____ on Pearl Harbor
KAZ	8. Foreman of the reservoir crew
ENDO	9. Mitsue ____ protested internment under habeas corpus & won
FISH	10. Mama worked at the ____ cannery
ELEVEN	11. Age of Jeanne's daughter when they went to the camp
DIETICIAN	12. Mama's job at the camp
CONGRESS	13. In 1924 immigration from Japan was stopped by US ____
DISLOYALTY	14. Greatest possible disgrace for a Japanese man to be charged with
ORCHARD	15. Spring of 1943 the family moved near the peach ____
CLOSED	16. December 5, 1945 Manzanar camp officially ____
KO	17. Papa's first name
OWENS	18. ____ Valley, CA; location of Manzanar camp
WOODY	19. Jeanne's older brother; drafted into the US Army; visited Japan
BUDDHIST	20. Family's religion

Farewell to Manzanar Fill In The Blank 4

_____ 1. Papa's job at Ft. Lincoln

_____ 2. Foreman of the reservoir crew

_____ 3. Jeanne's older brother; led a dance-band; sent to Germany

_____ 4. Papa's job before internment

_____ 5. Papa drafted plans to start one but never started it

_____ 6. Papa's first name

_____ 7. December 5, 1945 Manzanar camp officially _____

_____ 8. Mr. Tayama's first name; he was beaten at camp and almost died

_____ 9. Papa's version of the samurai sword

_____ 10. California city where first Japanese immigrants settled

_____ 11. Jeanne's elected position; Carnival _____

_____ 12. Several of Jeanne's family members moved to New ___ after the war

_____ 13. Mr. Kurihara; leader of Manzanar camp riot

_____ 14. ____ Homes; where the family lived after the war was over

_____ 15. December 7, 1941 was the date of the Japanese _____ on Pearl Harbor

_____ 16. Block 16 was the location of the first ____ the family lived in

_____ 17. Ka-Ke; Papa's home in _____

_____ 18. Executive Order 9066 allowed the military to _____ people from Western areas

_____ 19. Girl ___ did not accept Jeanne as a member

_____ 20. Jeanne thought it was a misuse of the body

Farewell to Manzanar Fill In The Blank 4 Answer Key

INTERVIEWER	1. Papa's job at Ft. Lincoln
KAZ	2. Foreman of the reservoir crew
BILL	3. Jeanne's older brother; led a dance-band; sent to Germany
FISHERMAN	4. Papa's job before internment
COOPERATIVE	5. Papa drafted plans to start one but never started it
KO	6. Papa's first name
CLOSED	7. December 5, 1945 Manzanar camp officially _____
FRED	8. Mr. Tayama's first name; he was beaten at camp and almost died
CANE	9. Papa's version of the samurai sword
SACRAMENTO	10. California city where first Japanese immigrants settled
QUEEN	11. Jeanne's elected position; Carnival _____
JERSEY	12. Several of Jeanne's family members moved to New ___ after the war
JOE	13. Mr. Kurihara; leader of Manzanar camp riot
CABRILLO	14. ____ Homes; where the family lived after the war was over
ATTACK	15. December 7, 1941 was the date of the Japanese _____ on Pearl Harbor
BARRACKS	16. Block 16 was the location of the first ____ the family lived in
JAPAN	17. Ka-Ke; Papa's home in _____
EXCLUDE	18. Executive Order 9066 allowed the military to _____ people from Western areas
SCOUTS	19. Girl ___ did not accept Jeanne as a member
BALLET	20. Jeanne thought it was a misuse of the body

Farewell to Manzanar Matching 1

___ 1. INLAND
___ 2. HIROSHIMA
___ 3. CHIZU
___ 4. JAPAN
___ 5. STRAWBERRIES
___ 6. OCEAN
___ 7. SHIG
___ 8. ENDO
___ 9. COMBAT
___ 10. JOE
___ 11. MANZANAR
___ 12. SURRENDER
___ 13. THOUSAND
___ 14. SCOUTS
___ 15. CITIZENS
___ 16. BALLET
___ 17. INTERVIEWER
___ 18. FAMILY
___ 19. OWENS
___ 20. HARBOR
___ 21. FRED
___ 22. BUDDHIST
___ 23. EXCLUDE
___ 24. JOSE
___ 25. RADINE

A. In 1952 the family moved to San Jose and Papa raised _____
B. Jeanne thought it was a misuse of the body
C. ____ Valley, CA; location of Manzanar camp
D. Pearl ___; American base in Hawaii bombed by Japan
E. Public Law 414 allowed Japanese-Americans to become US _____
F. Mr. Tayama's first name; he was beaten at camp and almost died
G. Eleanor's husband; drafted into US Army
H. Number of interned Japanese-Americans: 110 _____
I. August 12, 1942 Evacuation to ten ____ camps was completed
J. Woody's wife
K. Mitsue ___ protested internment under habeas corpus & won
L. Mess hall caused the disintegration of the _____
M. Mr. Kurihara; leader of Manzanar camp riot
N. Executive Order 9066 allowed the military to _____ people from Western areas
O. San ____; family home for Jeanne's last year in high school
P. Resettlement camp for Japanese Americans
Q. Papa's job at Ft. Lincoln
R. Girl ____ did not accept Jeanne as a member
S. August 6, 1945 US dropped atom bomb on _____
T. ____ Park; where Wakatsuki family lived before their internment
U. 442nd ____ Regiment was an all Nisei unit in the US Army
V. Family's religion
W. Jeanne's friend in junior high but not high school
X. August 14, 1945 Japan _____ed; WWII ended
Y. Ka-Ke; Papa's home in _____

Farewell to Manzanar Matching 1 Answer Key

I -	1. INLAND	A. In 1952 the family moved to San Jose and Papa raised _____
S -	2. HIROSHIMA	B. Jeanne thought it was a misuse of the body
J -	3. CHIZU	C. _____ Valley, CA; location of Manzanar camp
Y -	4. JAPAN	D. Pearl ___; American base in Hawaii bombed by Japan
A -	5. STRAWBERRIES	E. Public Law 414 allowed Japanese-Americans to become US _____
T -	6. OCEAN	F. Mr. Tayama's first name; he was beaten at camp and almost died
G -	7. SHIG	G. Eleanor's husband; drafted into US Army
K -	8. ENDO	H. Number of interned Japanese-Americans: 110 _____
U -	9. COMBAT	I. August 12, 1942 Evacuation to ten _____ camps was completed
M -	10. JOE	J. Woody's wife
P -	11. MANZANAR	K. Mitsue ___ protested internment under habeas corpus & won
X -	12. SURRENDER	L. Mess hall caused the disintegration of the _____
H -	13. THOUSAND	M. Mr. Kurihara; leader of Manzanar camp riot
R -	14. SCOUTS	N. Executive Order 9066 allowed the military to _____ people from Western areas
E -	15. CITIZENS	O. San ____; family home for Jeanne's last year in high school
B -	16. BALLET	P. Resettlement camp for Japanese Americans
Q -	17. INTERVIEWER	Q. Papa's job at Ft. Lincoln
L -	18. FAMILY	R. Girl ___ did not accept Jeanne as a member
C -	19. OWENS	S. August 6, 1945 US dropped atom bomb on _____
D -	20. HARBOR	T. ____ Park; where Wakatsuki family lived before their internment
F -	21. FRED	U. 442nd _____ Regiment was an all Nisei unit in the US Army
V -	22. BUDDHIST	V. Family's religion
N -	23. EXCLUDE	W. Jeanne's friend in junior high but not high school
O -	24. JOSE	X. August 14, 1945 Japan _____ed; WWII ended
W -	25. RADINE	Y. Ka-Ke; Papa's home in _____

Farewell to Manzanar Matching 2

___ 1. QUEEN   A. Public Law 414 allowed Japanese-Americans to become US _____
___ 2. CANE   B. ____ Park; where Wakatsuki family lived before their internment
___ 3. BUDDHIST   C. Papa drafted plans to start one but never started it
___ 4. MANZANAR   D. Mr. Tayama's first name; he was beaten at camp and almost died
___ 5. CATHOLIC   E. Religion to which Jeanne wanted to convert
___ 6. CLOSED   F. In 1952 the family moved to San Jose and Papa raised _____
___ 7. EXCLUDE   G. Family's religion
___ 8. FAMILY   H. Several of Jeanne's family members moved to New ___ after the war
___ 9. TOMI   I. Jeanne's older brother; drafted into the US Army; visited Japan
___ 10. INU   J. Number of months Papa spent at Ft. Lincoln
___ 11. STRAWBERRIES K. ____ Valley, CA; location of Manzanar camp
___ 12. NINE   L. Papa's job before internment
___ 13. CITIZENS   M. Ft. ____; Papa was imprisoned there
___ 14. FRED   N. Executive Order 9066 allowed the military to _____ people from Western areas
___ 15. OWENS   O. Bill's wife
___ 16. FISHERMAN   P. Papa's version of the samurai sword
___ 17. DISLOYALTY   Q. December 5, 1945 Manzanar camp officially _____
___ 18. JERSEY   R. Resettlement camp for Japanese Americans
___ 19. OCEAN   S. Traitor; women called Papa this
___ 20. LINCOLN   T. August 6, 1945 US dropped atom bomb on _____
___ 21. HIROSHIMA   U. Jeanne's elected position; Carnival _____
___ 22. WOODY   V. Greatest possible disgrace for a Japanese man to be charged with
___ 23. SCOUTS   W. Girl ___ did not accept Jeanne as a member
___ 24. KIYO   X. Jeanne's brother; punched Papa in the face to protect Mama
___ 25. COOPERATIVE Y. Mess hall caused the disintegration of the _____

Farewell to Manzanar Matching 2 Answer Key

U - 1. QUEEN	A. Public Law 414 allowed Japanese-Americans to become US _____
P - 2. CANE	B. ____ Park; where Wakatsuki family lived before their internment
G - 3. BUDDHIST	C. Papa drafted plans to start one but never started it
R - 4. MANZANAR	D. Mr. Tayama's first name; he was beaten at camp and almost died
E - 5. CATHOLIC	E. Religion to which Jeanne wanted to convert
Q - 6. CLOSED	F. In 1952 the family moved to San Jose and Papa raised _____
N - 7. EXCLUDE	G. Family's religion
Y - 8. FAMILY	H. Several of Jeanne's family members moved to New ____ after the war
O - 9. TOMI	I. Jeanne's older brother; drafted into the US Army; visited Japan
S - 10. INU	J. Number of months Papa spent at Ft. Lincoln
F - 11. STRAWBERRIES	K. ____ Valley, CA; location of Manzanar camp
J - 12. NINE	L. Papa's job before internment
A - 13. CITIZENS	M. Ft. ____; Papa was imprisoned there
D - 14. FRED	N. Executive Order 9066 allowed the military to _____ people from Western areas
K - 15. OWENS	O. Bill's wife
L - 16. FISHERMAN	P. Papa's version of the samurai sword
V - 17. DISLOYALTY	Q. December 5, 1945 Manzanar camp officially _____
H - 18. JERSEY	R. Resettlement camp for Japanese Americans
B - 19. OCEAN	S. Traitor; women called Papa this
M - 20. LINCOLN	T. August 6, 1945 US dropped atom bomb on _____
T - 21. HIROSHIMA	U. Jeanne's elected position; Carnival _____
I - 22. WOODY	V. Greatest possible disgrace for a Japanese man to be charged with
W - 23. SCOUTS	W. Girl ____ did not accept Jeanne as a member
X - 24. KIYO	X. Jeanne's brother; punched Papa in the face to protect Mama
C - 25. COOPERATIVE	Y. Mess hall caused the disintegration of the _____

Farewell to Manzanar Matching 3

___ 1. ELEVEN A. In 1886 the Japanese government lifted its ban on _____
___ 2. SURRENDER B. Jeanne's age when the family went to Manzanar
___ 3. CITIZENS C. Papa's job before internment
___ 4. RADINE D. August 14, 1945 Japan _____ed; WWII ended
___ 5. BALLET E. Mr. Kurihara; leader of Manzanar camp riot
___ 6. MANZANAR F. Jeanne thought it was a misuse of the body
___ 7. CLOSED G. In 1952 the family moved to San Jose and Papa raised _____
___ 8. BUDDHIST H. December 5, 1945 Manzanar camp officially _____
___ 9. WOODY I. In 1869 the first Japanese ____ arrived in the US
___ 10. IMMIGRANTS J. Age of Jeanne's daughter when they went to the camp
___ 11. ORCHARD K. Oath Japanese-American men were asked to sign
___ 12. JOE L. 442nd ____ Regiment was an all Nisei unit in the US Army
___ 13. KAZ M. Resettlement camp for Japanese Americans
___ 14. SEVEN N. Hirabayashi & Korematsu challenged racial bias of _____ order & lost
___ 15. BILL O. Papa's first name
___ 16. EVACUATION P. Spring of 1943 the family moved near the peach ____
___ 17. FISHERMAN Q. Public Law 414 allowed Japanese-Americans to become US _____
___ 18. COMBAT R. Foreman of the reservoir crew
___ 19. JERSEY S. Eleanor's husband; drafted into US Army
___ 20. EMIGRATION T. Jeanne's older brother; led a dance-band; sent to Germany
___ 21. ENGLISH U. Jeanne's older brother; drafted into the US Army; visited Japan
___ 22. KO V. Language Jeanne spoke
___ 23. SHIG W. Jeanne's friend in junior high but not high school
___ 24. LOYALTY X. Several of Jeanne's family members moved to New ___ after the war
___ 25. STRAWBERRIES Y. Family's religion

Farewell to Manzanar Matching 3 Answer Key

J - 1. ELEVEN	A. In 1886 the Japanese government lifted its ban on _____
D - 2. SURRENDER	B. Jeanne's age when the family went to Manzanar
Q - 3. CITIZENS	C. Papa's job before internment
W - 4. RADINE	D. August 14, 1945 Japan _____ed; WWII ended
F - 5. BALLET	E. Mr. Kurihara; leader of Manzanar camp riot
M - 6. MANZANAR	F. Jeanne thought it was a misuse of the body
H - 7. CLOSED	G. In 1952 the family moved to San Jose and Papa raised _____
Y - 8. BUDDHIST	H. December 5, 1945 Manzanar camp officially _____
U - 9. WOODY	I. In 1869 the first Japanese ____ arrived in the US
I - 10. IMMIGRANTS	J. Age of Jeanne's daughter when they went to the camp
P - 11. ORCHARD	K. Oath Japanese-American men were asked to sign
E - 12. JOE	L. 442nd ____ Regiment was an all Nisei unit in the US Army
R - 13. KAZ	M. Resettlement camp for Japanese Americans
B - 14. SEVEN	N. Hirabayashi & Korematsu challenged racial bias of _____ order & lost
T - 15. BILL	O. Papa's first name
N - 16. EVACUATION	P. Spring of 1943 the family moved near the peach ____
C - 17. FISHERMAN	Q. Public Law 414 allowed Japanese-Americans to become US _____
L - 18. COMBAT	R. Foreman of the reservoir crew
X - 19. JERSEY	S. Eleanor's husband; drafted into US Army
A - 20. EMIGRATION	T. Jeanne's older brother; led a dance-band; sent to Germany
V - 21. ENGLISH	U. Jeanne's older brother; drafted into the US Army; visited Japan
O - 22. KO	V. Language Jeanne spoke
S - 23. SHIG	W. Jeanne's friend in junior high but not high school
K - 24. LOYALTY	X. Several of Jeanne's family members moved to New ___ after the war
G - 25. STRAWBERRIES	Y. Family's religion

Farewell to Manzanar Matching 4

___ 1. HARBOR A. Papa drafted plans to start one but never started it
___ 2. INLAND B. Pearl ___; American base in Hawaii bombed by Japan
___ 3. CITIZENS C. 442nd ____ Regiment was an all Nisei unit in the US Army
___ 4. CONGRESS D. Mama worked at the ___ cannery
___ 5. EXCLUDE E. Woody's wife
___ 6. OCEAN F. August 12, 1942 Evacuation to ten ____ camps was completed
___ 7. JOSE G. California city where first Japanese immigrants settled
___ 8. CHIZU H. Number of years it took Jeanne to go back to Manzanar
___ 9. STRAWBERRIES I. ____ Valley, CA; location of Manzanar camp
___ 10. JAPAN J. Age of Jeanne's daughter when they went to the camp
___ 11. ENDO K. Executive Order 9066 allowed the military to _____ people from Western areas
___ 12. COMBAT L. Jeanne's elected position; Carnival _____
___ 13. COOPERATIVE M. ____ Park; where Wakatsuki family lived before their internment
___ 14. CLOSED N. December 5, 1945 Manzanar camp officially _____
___ 15. SURRENDER O. Public Law 414 allowed Japanese-Americans to become US _____
___ 16. ELEVEN P. Mitsue ___ protested internment under habeas corpus & won
___ 17. RADINE Q. Foreman of the reservoir crew
___ 18. QUEEN R. In 1952 the family moved to San Jose and Papa raised _____
___ 19. SACRAMENTO S. Jeanne's friend in junior high but not high school
___ 20. FISHERMAN T. August 14, 1945 Japan _____ed; WWII ended
___ 21. KAZ U. In 1924 immigration from Japan was stopped by US _____
___ 22. FISH V. San ____; family home for Jeanne's last year in high school
___ 23. BARRACKS W. Ka-Ke; Papa's home in _____
___ 24. OWENS X. Block 16 was the location of the first ____ the family lived in
___ 25. THIRTY Y. Papa's job before internment

Farewell to Manzanar Matching 4 Answer Key

B - 1. HARBOR	A. Papa drafted plans to start one but never started it
F - 2. INLAND	B. Pearl ___; American base in Hawaii bombed by Japan
O - 3. CITIZENS	C. 442nd ____ Regiment was an all Nisei unit in the US Army
U - 4. CONGRESS	D. Mama worked at the ___ cannery
K - 5. EXCLUDE	E. Woody's wife
M - 6. OCEAN	F. August 12, 1942 Evacuation to ten ____ camps was completed
V - 7. JOSE	G. California city where first Japanese immigrants settled
E - 8. CHIZU	H. Number of years it took Jeanne to go back to Manzanar
R - 9. STRAWBERRIES	I. ____ Valley, CA; location of Manzanar camp
W - 10. JAPAN	J. Age of Jeanne's daughter when they went to the camp
P - 11. ENDO	K. Executive Order 9066 allowed the military to _____ people from Western areas
C - 12. COMBAT	L. Jeanne's elected position; Carnival _____
A - 13. COOPERATIVE	M. ____ Park; where Wakatsuki family lived before their internment
N - 14. CLOSED	N. December 5, 1945 Manzanar camp officially _____
T - 15. SURRENDER	O. Public Law 414 allowed Japanese-Americans to become US _____
J - 16. ELEVEN	P. Mitsue ___ protested internment under habeas corpus & won
S - 17. RADINE	Q. Foreman of the reservoir crew
L - 18. QUEEN	R. In 1952 the family moved to San Jose and Papa raised _____
G - 19. SACRAMENTO	S. Jeanne's friend in junior high but not high school
Y - 20. FISHERMAN	T. August 14, 1945 Japan _____ed; WWII ended
Q - 21. KAZ	U. In 1924 immigration from Japan was stopped by US _____
D - 22. FISH	V. San ____; family home for Jeanne's last year in high school
X - 23. BARRACKS	W. Ka-Ke; Papa's home in _____
I - 24. OWENS	X. Block 16 was the location of the first ____ the family lived in
H - 25. THIRTY	Y. Papa's job before internment

Farewell to Manzanar Magic Squares 1

Match the definition with the vocabulary word. Put your answers in the magic squares below. When your answers are correct, all columns and rows will add to the same number.

A. TERMINAL
B. CONGRESS
C. SEVEN
D. FISH
E. BALLET
F. HARBOR
G. KAZ
H. MANZANAR
I. ORCHARD
J. KIYO
K. IMMIGRANTS
L. JERSEY
M. STRAWBERRIES
N. CITIZENS
O. ENGLISH
P. NASH

1. Long Beach was the location of _____ Island
2. Public Law 414 allowed Japanese-Americans to become US _____
3. Jeanne's brother; punched Papa in the face to protect Mama
4. Jeanne thought it was a misuse of the body
5. Foreman of the reservoir crew
6. Several of Jeanne's family members moved to New ___ after the war
7. Model of car Papa drove out of Manzanar
8. Jeanne's age when the family went to Manzanar
9. Language Jeanne spoke
10. Mama worked at the ___ cannery
11. Resettlement camp for Japanese Americans
12. In 1869 the first Japanese ____ arrived in the US
13. Spring of 1943 the family moved near the peach ____
14. Pearl ___; American base in Hawaii bombed by Japan
15. In 1924 immigration from Japan was stopped by US _____
16. In 1952 the family moved to San Jose and Papa raised _____

A=	B=	C=	D=
E=	F=	G=	H=
I=	J=	K=	L=
M=	N=	O=	P=

22
Copyrighted

Farewell to Manzanar Magic Squares 1 Answer Key

Match the definition with the vocabulary word. Put your answers in the magic squares below. When your answers are correct, all columns and rows will add to the same number.

A. TERMINAL
B. CONGRESS
C. SEVEN
D. FISH
E. BALLET
F. HARBOR
G. KAZ
H. MANZANAR
I. ORCHARD
J. KIYO
K. IMMIGRANTS
L. JERSEY
M. STRAWBERRIES
N. CITIZENS
O. ENGLISH
P. NASH

1. Long Beach was the location of _____ Island
2. Public Law 414 allowed Japanese-Americans to become US _____
3. Jeanne's brother; punched Papa in the face to protect Mama
4. Jeanne thought it was a misuse of the body
5. Foreman of the reservoir crew
6. Several of Jeanne's family members moved to New ___ after the war
7. Model of car Papa drove out of Manzanar
8. Jeanne's age when the family went to Manzanar
9. Language Jeanne spoke
10. Mama worked at the ___ cannery
11. Resettlement camp for Japanese Americans
12. In 1869 the first Japanese ____ arrived in the US
13. Spring of 1943 the family moved near the peach ____
14. Pearl ___; American base in Hawaii bombed by Japan
15. In 1924 immigration from Japan was stopped by US _____
16. In 1952 the family moved to San Jose and Papa raised _____

A=1	B=15	C=8	D=10
E=4	F=14	G=5	H=11
I=13	J=3	K=12	L=6
M=16	N=2	O=9	P=7

23
Copyrighted

Farewell to Manzanar Magic Squares 2

Match the definition with the vocabulary word. Put your answers in the magic squares below. When your answers are correct, all columns and rows will add to the same number.

A. SEVEN
B. SCOUTS
C. SACRAMENTO
D. INTERVIEWER
E. WOODY
F. FRED
G. ENDO
H. EMIGRATION
I. EVACUATION
J. EXCLUDE
K. LOYALTY
L. BARRACKS
M. KO
N. OWENS
O. COMBAT
P. INLAND

1. In 1886 the Japanese government lifted its ban on _____
2. Papa's first name
3. Girl ___ did not accept Jeanne as a member
4. Oath Japanese-American men were asked to sign
5. Executive Order 9066 allowed the military to _____ people from Western areas
6. California city where first Japanese immigrants settled
7. August 12, 1942 Evacuation to ten ____ camps was completed
8. Jeanne's older brother; drafted into the US Army; visited Japan
9. 442nd ____ Regiment was an all Nisei unit in the US Army
10. Mr. Tayama's first name; he was beaten at camp and almost died
11. Hirabayashi & Korematsu challenged racial bias of _____ order & lost
12. Papa's job at Ft. Lincoln
13. Jeanne's age when the family went to Manzanar
14. Block 16 was the location of the first ____ the family lived in
15. Mitsue ___ protested internment under habeas corpus & won
16. ____ Valley, CA; location of Manzanar camp

A=13	B=3	C=6	D=12
E=8	F=10	G=15	H=1
I=11	J=5	K=4	L=14
M=2	N=16	O=9	P=7

Farewell to Manzanar Magic Squares 2 Answer Key

Match the definition with the vocabulary word. Put your answers in the magic squares below. When your answers are correct, all columns and rows will add to the same number.

A. SEVEN
B. SCOUTS
C. SACRAMENTO
D. INTERVIEWER
E. WOODY
F. FRED
G. ENDO
H. EMIGRATION
I. EVACUATION
J. EXCLUDE
K. LOYALTY
L. BARRACKS
M. KO
N. OWENS
O. COMBAT
P. INLAND

1. In 1886 the Japanese government lifted its ban on _____
2. Papa's first name
3. Girl ___ did not accept Jeanne as a member
4. Oath Japanese-American men were asked to sign
5. Executive Order 9066 allowed the military to _____ people from Western areas
6. California city where first Japanese immigrants settled
7. August 12, 1942 Evacuation to ten ____ camps was completed
8. Jeanne's older brother; drafted into the US Army; visited Japan
9. 442nd ____ Regiment was an all Nisei unit in the US Army
10. Mr. Tayama's first name; he was beaten at camp and almost died
11. Hirabayashi & Korematsu challenged racial bias of _____ order & lost
12. Papa's job at Ft. Lincoln
13. Jeanne's age when the family went to Manzanar
14. Block 16 was the location of the first ____ the family lived in
15. Mitsue ___ protested internment under habeas corpus & won
16. ____ Valley, CA; location of Manzanar camp

A=13	B=3	C=6	D=12
E=8	F=10	G=15	H=1
I=11	J=5	K=4	L=14
M=2	N=16	O=9	P=7

Farewell to Manzanar Magic Squares 3

Match the definition with the vocabulary word. Put your answers in the magic squares below. When your answers are correct, all columns and rows will add to the same number.

A. HARBOR
B. NASH
C. CHIZU
D. LINCOLN
E. TOMI
F. SACRAMENTO
G. MANZANAR
H. FAMILY
I. ELEANOR
J. BILL
K. COOPERATIVE
L. BALLET
M. CONGRESS
N. OCEAN
O. ENGLISH
P. DIETICIAN

1. In 1924 immigration from Japan was stopped by US _____
2. California city where first Japanese immigrants settled
3. Mess hall caused the disintegration of the _____
4. Language Jeanne spoke
5. Jeanne thought it was a misuse of the body
6. Woody's wife
7. Pearl ___; American base in Hawaii bombed by Japan
8. Jeanne's older brother; led a dance-band; sent to Germany
9. Papa drafted plans to start one but never started it
10. Ft. ____; Papa was imprisoned there
11. Model of car Papa drove out of Manzanar
12. Jeanne's older sister; re-entered camp; had a baby in camp
13. ____ Park; where Wakatsuki family lived before their internment
14. Bill's wife
15. Resettlement camp for Japanese Americans
16. Mama's job at the camp

A=	B=	C=	D=
E=	F=	G=	H=
I=	J=	K=	L=
M=	N=	O=	P=

Farewell to Manzanar Magic Squares 3 Answer Key

Match the definition with the vocabulary word. Put your answers in the magic squares below. When your answers are correct, all columns and rows will add to the same number.

A. HARBOR
B. NASH
C. CHIZU
D. LINCOLN
E. TOMI
F. SACRAMENTO
G. MANZANAR
H. FAMILY
I. ELEANOR
J. BILL
K. COOPERATIVE
L. BALLET
M. CONGRESS
N. OCEAN
O. ENGLISH
P. DIETICIAN

1. In 1924 immigration from Japan was stopped by US _____
2. California city where first Japanese immigrants settled
3. Mess hall caused the disintegration of the _____
4. Language Jeanne spoke
5. Jeanne thought it was a misuse of the body
6. Woody's wife
7. Pearl ___; American base in Hawaii bombed by Japan
8. Jeanne's older brother; led a dance-band; sent to Germany
9. Papa drafted plans to start one but never started it
10. Ft. ____; Papa was imprisoned there
11. Model of car Papa drove out of Manzanar
12. Jeanne's older sister; re-entered camp; had a baby in camp
13. ____ Park; where Wakatsuki family lived before their internment
14. Bill's wife
15. Resettlement camp for Japanese Americans
16. Mama's job at the camp

A=7	B=11	C=6	D=10
E=14	F=2	G=15	H=3
I=12	J=8	K=9	L=5
M=1	N=13	O=4	P=16

Farewell to Manzanar Magic Squares 4

Match the definition with the vocabulary word. Put your answers in the magic squares below. When your answers are correct, all columns and rows will add to the same number.

A. KIYO
B. FISH
C. COMBAT
D. CABRILLO
E. BUDDHIST
F. INTERVIEWER
G. TERMINAL
H. NINE
I. CONGRESS
J. HIROSHIMA
K. SHIG
L. EMIGRATION
M. WOODY
N. OWENS
O. CHIZU
P. TOMI

1. Woody's wife
2. ____ Homes; where the family lived after the war was over
3. August 6, 1945 US dropped atom bomb on _____
4. Family's religion
5. In 1924 immigration from Japan was stopped by US _____
6. Papa's job at Ft. Lincoln
7. Bill's wife
8. 442nd ____ Regiment was an all Nisei unit in the US Army
9. Number of months Papa spent at Ft. Lincoln
10. Eleanor's husband; drafted into US Army
11. Jeanne's brother; punched Papa in the face to protect Mama
12. ____ Valley, CA; location of Manzanar camp
13. Mama worked at the ___ cannery
14. Jeanne's older brother; drafted into the US Army; visited Japan
15. Long Beach was the location of _____ Island
16. In 1886 the Japanese government lifted its ban on _____

A=	B=	C=	D=
E=	F=	G=	H=
I=	J=	K=	L=
M=	N=	O=	P=

Farewell to Manzanar Magic Squares 4 Answer Key

Match the definition with the vocabulary word. Put your answers in the magic squares below. When your answers are correct, all columns and rows will add to the same number.

A. KIYO
B. FISH
C. COMBAT
D. CABRILLO
E. BUDDHIST
F. INTERVIEWER
G. TERMINAL
H. NINE
I. CONGRESS
J. HIROSHIMA
K. SHIG
L. EMIGRATION
M. WOODY
N. OWENS
O. CHIZU
P. TOMI

1. Woody's wife
2. ____ Homes; where the family lived after the war was over
3. August 6, 1945 US dropped atom bomb on _____
4. Family's religion
5. In 1924 immigration from Japan was stopped by US _____
6. Papa's job at Ft. Lincoln
7. Bill's wife
8. 442nd ____ Regiment was an all Nisei unit in the US Army
9. Number of months Papa spent at Ft. Lincoln
10. Eleanor's husband; drafted into US Army
11. Jeanne's brother; punched Papa in the face to protect Mama
12. ____ Valley, CA; location of Manzanar camp
13. Mama worked at the ___ cannery
14. Jeanne's older brother; drafted into the US Army; visited Japan
15. Long Beach was the location of _____ Island
16. In 1886 the Japanese government lifted its ban on _____

A=11	B=13	C=8	D=2
E=4	F=6	G=15	H=9
I=5	J=3	K=10	L=16
M=14	N=12	O=1	P=7

Copyrighted

Farewell to Manzanar Word Search 1

```
E N S J G W T K Y T D N L S J B Z L H J
N Q F P N N H T B Z N Y W L M F V I S R
G T H E C K O X T O S C S O X C G N T D
L S V C F P U Q I Z H D L M O H N C R F
I E L A P W S T H T R T J O I D P O A X
S O T N E M A R C A S J E R S E Y L W G
H N I E K R N G H I V D O X Z E A N B F
W N X K G Z D C H Q B S K V C N D M E M
E W J I T C R D Q F H A R I I L Z X R G
R J M J E O D H K I R T R M N Q U S R C
Z E W S L U W C M O Z E R R U L S D I Y
C F O M B R A A N G J E D E A E A D E S
V J Y Z V T Y A Y N T L E Z R C F N S Z
N T I C T M E F I S H N R G Y Q K M D B
L F K A S L K H Z B H R N V V G W S Q F
J Q G V E D S F P P X O T T D V Z W W R
L G L W X B S G D G C S P C N Q R G R V
C H I Z U D I E T I C I A N P L L Z W R
M A N Z A N A R G Q L F X K H V L P C V
```

August 12, 1942 Evacuation to ten ____ camps was completed (6)
August 6, 1945 US dropped atom bomb on _____ (9)
Block 16 was the location of the first ____ the family lived in (8)
California city where first Japanese immigrants settled (10)
December 5, 1945 Manzanar camp officially _____ (6)
December 7, 1941 was the date of the Japanese _____ on Pearl Harbor (6)
Executive Order 9066 allowed the military to _____ people from Western areas (7)
Family's religion (8)
Ft. ____; Papa was imprisoned there (7)
In 1924 immigration from Japan was stopped by US _____ (8)
In 1952 the family moved to San Jose and Papa raised _____ (12)
Jeanne's age when the family went to Manzanar (5)
Jeanne's brother; punched Papa in the face to protect Mama (4)
Jeanne's elected position; Carnival _____ (5)
Jeanne's older brother; drafted into the US Army; visited Japan (5)
Jeanne's older sister; re-entered camp; had a baby in camp (7)
Language Jeanne spoke (7)
Long Beach was the location of _____ Island (8)
Mama worked at the ___ cannery (4)
Mama's job at the camp (9)
Mr. Tayama's first name; he was beaten at camp and almost died (4)
Number of interned Japanese-Americans: 110 _____ (8)
Number of months Papa spent at Ft. Lincoln (4)
Papa's version of the samurai sword (4)
Resettlement camp for Japanese Americans (8)
San ____; family home for Jeanne's last year in high school (4)
Several of Jeanne's family members moved to New ___ after the war (6)
Spring of 1943 the family moved near the peach _____ (7)
Traitor; women called Papa this (3)
Woody's wife (5)
In 1886 the Japanese government lifted its ban on _____ (10)

Farewell to Manzanar Word Search 1 Answer Key

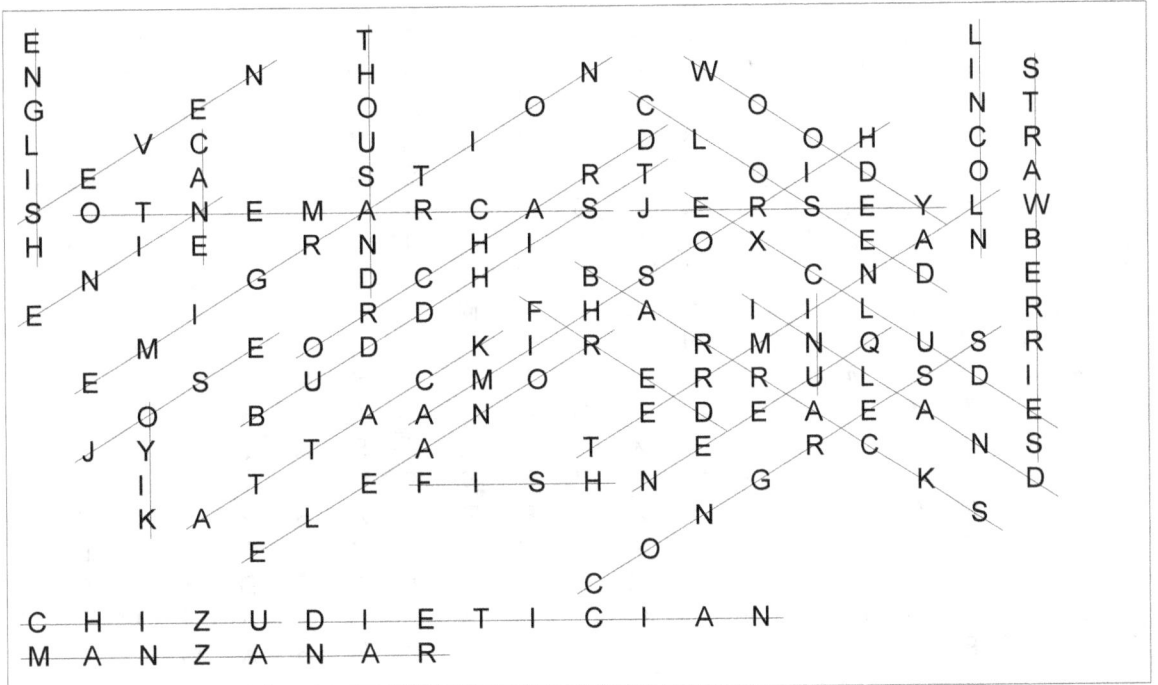

August 12, 1942 Evacuation to ten ____ camps was completed (6)

August 6, 1945 US dropped atom bomb on _____ (9)

Block 16 was the location of the first ____ the family lived in (8)

California city where first Japanese immigrants settled (10)

December 5, 1945 Manzanar camp officially _____ (6)

December 7, 1941 was the date of the Japanese _____ on Pearl Harbor (6)

Executive Order 9066 allowed the military to _____ people from Western areas (7)

Family's religion (8)

Ft. ____; Papa was imprisoned there (7)

In 1924 immigration from Japan was stopped by US _____ (8)

In 1952 the family moved to San Jose and Papa raised _____ (12)

Jeanne's age when the family went to Manzanar (5)

Jeanne's brother; punched Papa in the face to protect Mama (4)

Jeanne's elected position; Carnival _____ (5)

Jeanne's older brother; drafted into the US Army; visited Japan (5)

Jeanne's older sister; re-entered camp; had a baby in camp (7)

Language Jeanne spoke (7)

Long Beach was the location of _____ Island (8)

Mama worked at the ___ cannery (4)

Mama's job at the camp (9)

Mr. Tayama's first name; he was beaten at camp and almost died (4)

Number of interned Japanese-Americans: 110 _____ (8)

Number of months Papa spent at Ft. Lincoln (4)

Papa's version of the samurai sword (4)

Resettlement camp for Japanese Americans (8)

San ____; family home for Jeanne's last year in high school (4)

Several of Jeanne's family members moved to New ___ after the war (6)

Spring of 1943 the family moved near the peach _____ (7)

Traitor; women called Papa this (3)

Woody's wife (5)

In 1886 the Japanese government lifted its ban on _____ (10)

Farewell to Manzanar Word Search 2

```
C O M B A T I N T E R V I E W E R Q O H
Q K P P S H N C S N W S Z G N T S L N P
J Y F V H S I S U R R E N D E R L C N Y
B W L T S L T C S Z L B G H K I P G V G
P H M N O Q M F S P G H W S R B B B G Q
F B T H F M S A K D S Y Z B M A T F L Y
N Q T H G M K M X L T S A R Q L K T R M
N A M R E H S I F L J C R T J L X O B E
C W S K Y H V L A D A O M M O E Y M V S
S N T H I R T Y N S P R C Y E T D I K F
T H J S B M O E T Y A T T E S W T O A D
M O I Z K L V U T N N L Q J A A S H Z K
W W F G S E O Y Y X A N Q T R N G H T H
E E C I L C J R T Y B S N E Z I T I C N
Z N D E S B O L O Z B P P T Z B V K K K
Y S D P J B R L G W G O W X S F C N T D
K D J O R S L Y C G O X Y X T C D R T C
N D R A D I N E F C I M M I G R A N T S
G G H P B E V A C U A T I O N B X M G N
```

442nd ____ Regiment was an all Nisei unit in the US Army (6)

Age of Jeanne's daughter when they went to the camp (6)

August 14, 1945 Japan _____ ed; WWII ended (9)

Bill's wife (4)

Eleanor's husband; drafted into US Army (4)

Foreman of the reservoir crew (3)

Girl ___ did not accept Jeanne as a member (6)

Greatest possible disgrace for a Japanese man to be charged with (10)

Hirabayashi & Korematsu challenged racial bias of _____ order & lost (10)

In 1869 the first Japanese ____ arrived in the US (10)

Jeanne thought it was a misuse of the body (6)

Jeanne's friend in junior high but not high school (6)

Jeanne's older brother; led a dance-band; sent to Germany (4)

Ka-Ke; Papa's home in _____ (5)

Mess hall caused the disintegration of the _____ (6)

Mitsue ___ protested internment under habeas corpus & won (4)

Model of car Papa drove out of Manzanar (4)

Mr. Kurihara; leader of Manzanar camp riot (3)

Number of years it took Jeanne to go back to Manzanar (6)

Oath Japanese-American men were asked to sign (7)

Papa drafted plans to start one but never started it (11)

Papa's first name (2)

Papa's job at Ft. Lincoln (11)

Papa's job before internment (9)

Pearl ___; American base in Hawaii bombed by Japan (6)

Public Law 414 allowed Japanese-Americans to become US _____ (8)

Religion to which Jeanne wanted to convert (8)

____ Homes; where the family lived after the war was over (8)

____ Park; where Wakatsuki family lived before their internment (5)

____ Valley, CA; location of Manzanar camp (5)

Farewell to Manzanar Word Search 2 Answer Key

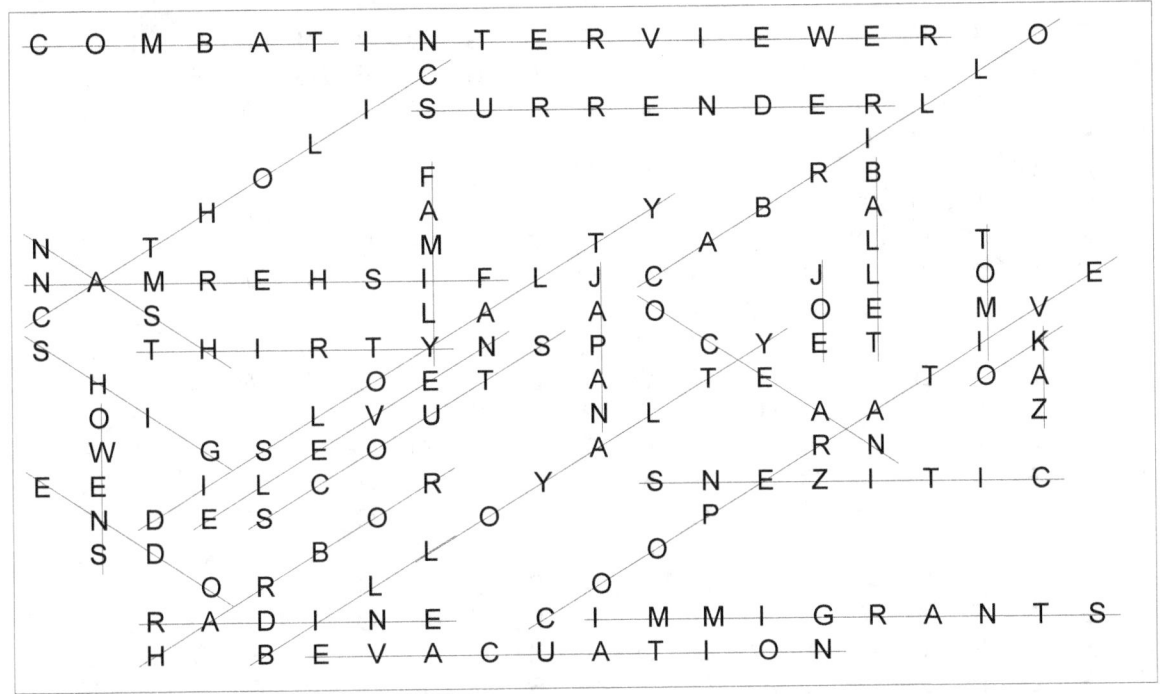

442nd ____ Regiment was an all Nisei unit in the US Army (6)
Age of Jeanne's daughter when they went to the camp (6)
August 14, 1945 Japan _____ed; WWII ended (9)
Bill's wife (4)
Eleanor's husband; drafted into US Army (4)
Foreman of the reservoir crew (3)
Girl ___ did not accept Jeanne as a member (6)
Greatest possible disgrace for a Japanese man to be charged with (10)
Hirabayashi & Korematsu challenged racial bias of _____ order & lost (10)
In 1869 the first Japanese ____ arrived in the US (10)
Jeanne thought it was a misuse of the body (6)
Jeanne's friend in junior high but not high school (6)
Jeanne's older brother; led a dance-band; sent to Germany (4)
Ka-Ke; Papa's home in _____ (5)
Mess hall caused the disintegration of the _____ (6)
Mitsue ___ protested internment under habeas corpus & won (4)
Model of car Papa drove out of Manzanar (4)
Mr. Kurihara; leader of Manzanar camp riot (3)
Number of years it took Jeanne to go back to Manzanar (6)
Oath Japanese-American men were asked to sign (7)
Papa drafted plans to start one but never started it (11)
Papa's first name (2)
Papa's job at Ft. Lincoln (11)
Papa's job before internment (9)
Pearl ___; American base in Hawaii bombed by Japan (6)
Public Law 414 allowed Japanese-Americans to become US _____ (8)
Religion to which Jeanne wanted to convert (8)
____ Homes; where the family lived after the war was over (8)
____ Park; where Wakatsuki family lived before their internment (5)
____ Valley, CA; location of Manzanar camp (5)

Farewell to Manzanar Word Search 3

```
S T R A W B E R R I E S S Q Y N J N H H
K D I S L O Y A L T Y G S H E G F B S C
S U R R E N D E R J K C V I I W I I J
S S Y T I H T W M X E F S G L T F W
C A W R N O Y G Y U N S H Y G I C H K
L V C E N T R O O E D J E H N Z V K P G
O W Q R L P W C W L J R N E P I R T W
S G H A A C S B H E M Y A N O W M H L R
E D Y I M M I G R A N T S K I Y O T E V
D O L N R Z E S N N R S H U A U T O N
L C I T B O E N F O N D N Y S Z W Q D Y
A H M E I Y S L T R B I C A N E M U O C
T I A R L C C H I O E A N O S O A E E P
T Z F V L M G K I N C D L E M J N E I K
A U I I N Q G B G M C E N L G B Z N L Q
C J N E V E L E F N A O A K E T A J O L
K O L W B A R R A C K S L N H T N T H P
Z S A E Z V N P S S E R G N O C A Q T A
K E N R Y H A R B O R Z O L L I R B A C
F S D H J J C O O P E R A T I V E M C K
```

ATTACK   ELEANOR   JAPAN   OWENS
BALLET   ELEVEN   JERSEY   QUEEN
BARRACKS   ENDO   JOE   RADINE
BILL   ENGLISH   JOSE   SACRAMENTO
CABRILLO   FAMILY   KAZ   SCOUTS
CANE   FISH   KIYO   SEVEN
CATHOLIC   FISHERMAN   KO   SHIG
CHIZU   FRED   LINCOLN   STRAWBERRIES
CITIZENS   HARBOR   LOYALTY   SURRENDER
CLOSED   HIROSHIMA   MANZANAR   THIRTY
COMBAT   IMMIGRANTS   NASH   THOUSAND
CONGRESS   INLAND   NINE   TOMI
COOPERATIVE   INTERVIEWER   OCEAN   WOODY
DISLOYALTY   INU   ORCHARD

Farewell to Manzanar Word Search 3 Answer Key

ATTACK	ELEANOR	JAPAN	OWENS
BALLET	ELEVEN	JERSEY	QUEEN
BARRACKS	ENDO	JOE	RADINE
BILL	ENGLISH	JOSE	SACRAMENTO
CABRILLO	FAMILY	KAZ	SCOUTS
CANE	FISH	KIYO	SEVEN
CATHOLIC	FISHERMAN	KO	SHIG
CHIZU	FRED	LINCOLN	STRAWBERRIES
CITIZENS	HARBOR	LOYALTY	SURRENDER
CLOSED	HIROSHIMA	MANZANAR	THIRTY
COMBAT	IMMIGRANTS	NASH	THOUSAND
CONGRESS	INLAND	NINE	TOMI
COOPERATIVE	INTERVIEWER	OCEAN	WOODY
DISLOYALTY	INU	ORCHARD	

Farewell to Manzanar Word Search 4

```
H A R B O R W Q G C R Y T B B I L L M S
S C O U T S P U R J L Z L A G T T Y M J P
S E V E N F F E F N K O B L B O X M F A Y
T C C J G I Y D R K T S L N M S T A G V
K I Y O H S A N S Y E S R E J I T H M T
J T T E Y H A N T R Z D M T D A S O I T
D S R L M L E M B N I R G B I I U L G
S P I N N W A I H I G C W M L E H S Y L
U D H I O Y N S N R A K O G S N D A D X
R I T Q O A T E A T S C N C O I D N O H
R E G L L T V T H C E E O I E D U D O V
E T S T C E I O N J R R T N H A B J W Q
N I C X L O L I N U P A V J G R N K A Z
D C A E N I X E S L U D M I A R X F Z Q
E I N D C M D J V C W M G E E P E Z N F
R A E R P U R C A C H I Z U N W A S Q G
E N D O L X C V A T T A C K V T E N S C
R Y F C E L E A N O R A M I H S O R I H
M L X B A R R A C K S F N L O C N I L B
S E O R C H A R D F J H G J P D B M Y R
```

ATTACK	DIETICIAN	FRED	KIYO	SACRAMENTO
BALLET	DISLOYALTY	HARBOR	KO	SCOUTS
BARRACKS	ELEANOR	HIROSHIMA	LINCOLN	SEVEN
BILL	ELEVEN	INLAND	LOYALTY	SHIG
BUDDHIST	EMIGRATION	INTERVIEWER	NASH	SURRENDER
CANE	ENDO	INU	NINE	TERMINAL
CATHOLIC	ENGLISH	JAPAN	OCEAN	THIRTY
CHIZU	EVACUATION	JERSEY	ORCHARD	THOUSAND
CLOSED	EXCLUDE	JOE	OWENS	TOMI
COMBAT	FAMILY	JOSE	QUEEN	WOODY
CONGRESS	FISH	KAZ	RADINE	

Farewell to Manzanar Word Search 4 Answer Key

ATTACK	DIETICIAN	FRED	KIYO	SACRAMENTO
BALLET	DISLOYALTY	HARBOR	KO	SCOUTS
BARRACKS	ELEANOR	HIROSHIMA	LINCOLN	SEVEN
BILL	ELEVEN	INLAND	LOYALTY	SHIG
BUDDHIST	EMIGRATION	INTERVIEWER	NASH	SURRENDER
CANE	ENDO	INU	NINE	TERMINAL
CATHOLIC	ENGLISH	JAPAN	OCEAN	THIRTY
CHIZU	EVACUATION	JERSEY	ORCHARD	THOUSAND
CLOSED	EXCLUDE	JOE	OWENS	TOMI
COMBAT	FAMILY	JOSE	QUEEN	WOODY
CONGRESS	FISH	KAZ	RADINE	

Farewell to Manzanar Crossword 1

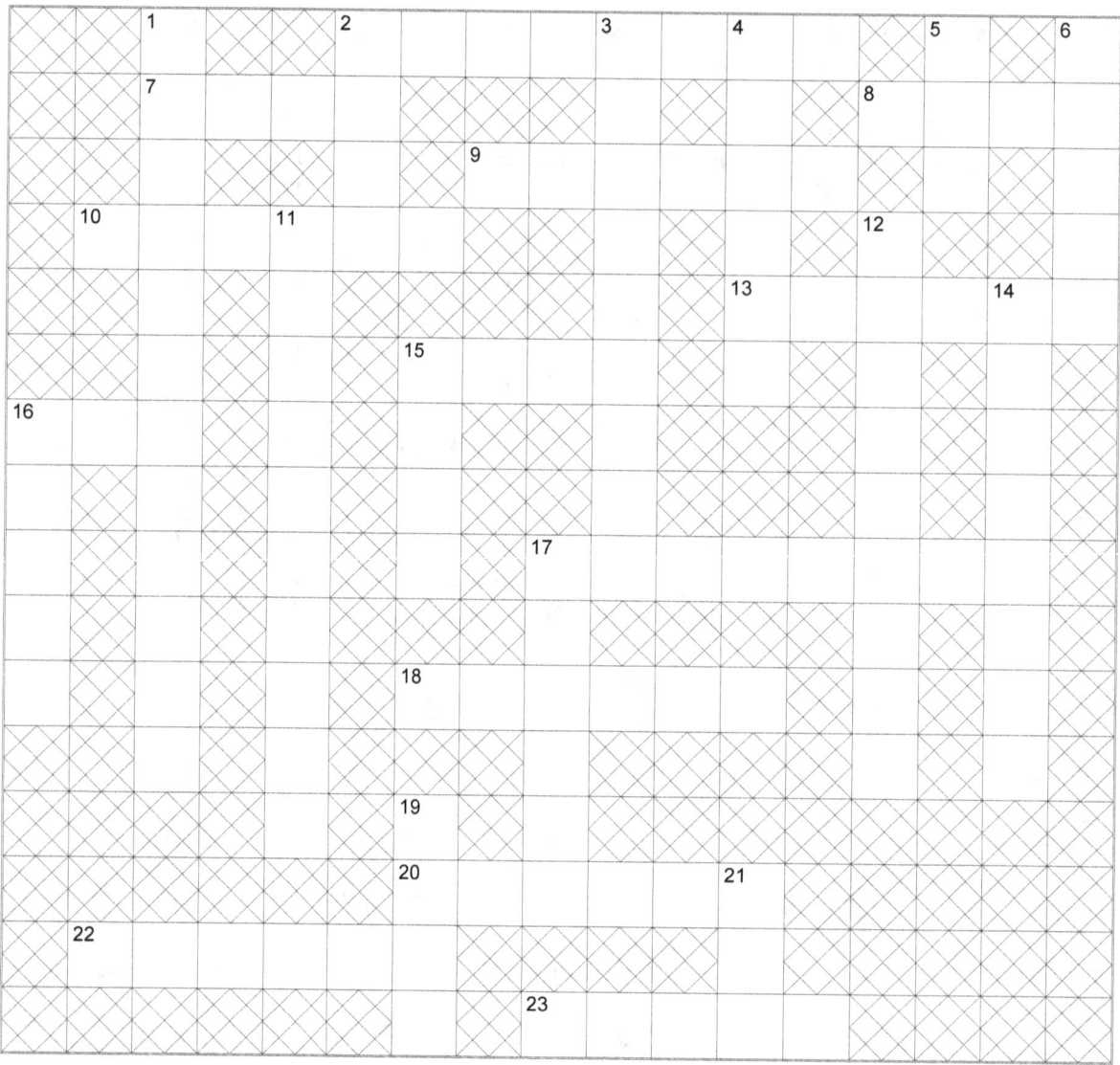

Across
2. Family's religion
7. Bill's wife
8. Mitsue ___ protested internment under habeas corpus & won
9. Pearl ___; American base in Hawaii bombed by Japan
10. Mess hall caused the disintegration of the ___
13. Number of years it took Jeanne to go back to Manzanar
15. Mama worked at the ___ cannery
16. Mr. Kurihara; leader of Manzanar camp riot
17. Block 16 was the location of the first ___ the family lived in
18. August 12, 1942 Evacuation to ten ___ camps was completed
20. December 7, 1941 was the date of the Japanese ___ on Pearl Harbor
22. Age of Jeanne's daughter when they went to the camp
23. Woody's wife

Down
1. In 1952 the family moved to San Jose and Papa raised ___
2. Jeanne's older brother; led a dance-band; sent to Germany
3. August 6, 1945 US dropped atom bomb on ___
4. Girl ___ did not accept Jeanne as a member
5. Traitor; women called Papa this
6. Jeanne's older brother; drafted into the US Army; visited Japan
11. In 1869 the first Japanese ___ arrived in the US
12. Mama's job at the camp
14. Number of interned Japanese-Americans: 110 ___
15. Mr. Tayama's first name; he was beaten at camp and almost died
16. Ka-Ke; Papa's home in ___
17. Jeanne thought it was a misuse of the body
19. Papa's version of the samurai sword
21. Foreman of the reservoir crew

Farewell to Manzanar Crossword 1 Answer Key

		1 S		2 B	U	D	D	3 H	I	4 S	T		5 I		6 W
		7 T	O	M	I			I		C		8 E	N	D	O
		R					9 H	A	R	B	O	R			O
	10 F	A	11 M	I	L	Y		O		U		12 D			D
		W		M				S		13 T	H	I	R	14 T	Y
		B		M		15 F	I	S	H	S		E		H	
16 J	O	E		I		R		I				T		O	
A		R		G		E		M				I		U	
P		R		R		D		17 B	A	R	R	A	C	K	S
A		I		A				A						A	
N		E		N		18 I	N	L	A	N	D		A		N
		S		T				L					N		D
				S		19 C	E								
						20 A	T	T	A	C	K	21			
		22 E	L	E	V	E	N					A			
						E		23 C	H	I	Z	U			

Across
2. Family's religion
7. Bill's wife
8. Mitsue ___ protested internment under habeas corpus & won
9. Pearl ___; American base in Hawaii bombed by Japan
10. Mess hall caused the disintegration of the ___
13. Number of years it took Jeanne to go back to Manzanar
15. Mama worked at the ___ cannery
16. Mr. Kurihara; leader of Manzanar camp riot
17. Block 16 was the location of the first ___ the family lived in
18. August 12, 1942 Evacuation to ten ___ camps was completed
20. December 7, 1941 was the date of the Japanese ___ on Pearl Harbor
22. Age of Jeanne's daughter when they went to the camp
23. Woody's wife

Down
1. In 1952 the family moved to San Jose and Papa raised ___
2. Jeanne's older brother; led a dance-band; sent to Germany
3. August 6, 1945 US dropped atom bomb on ___
4. Girl ___ did not accept Jeanne as a member
5. Traitor; women called Papa this
6. Jeanne's older brother; drafted into the US Army; visited Japan
11. In 1869 the first Japanese ___ arrived in the US
12. Mama's job at the camp
14. Number of interned Japanese-Americans: 110 ___
15. Mr. Tayama's first name; he was beaten at camp and almost died
16. Ka-Ke; Papa's home in ___
17. Jeanne thought it was a misuse of the body
19. Papa's version of the samurai sword
21. Foreman of the reservoir crew

Farewell to Manzanar Crossword 2

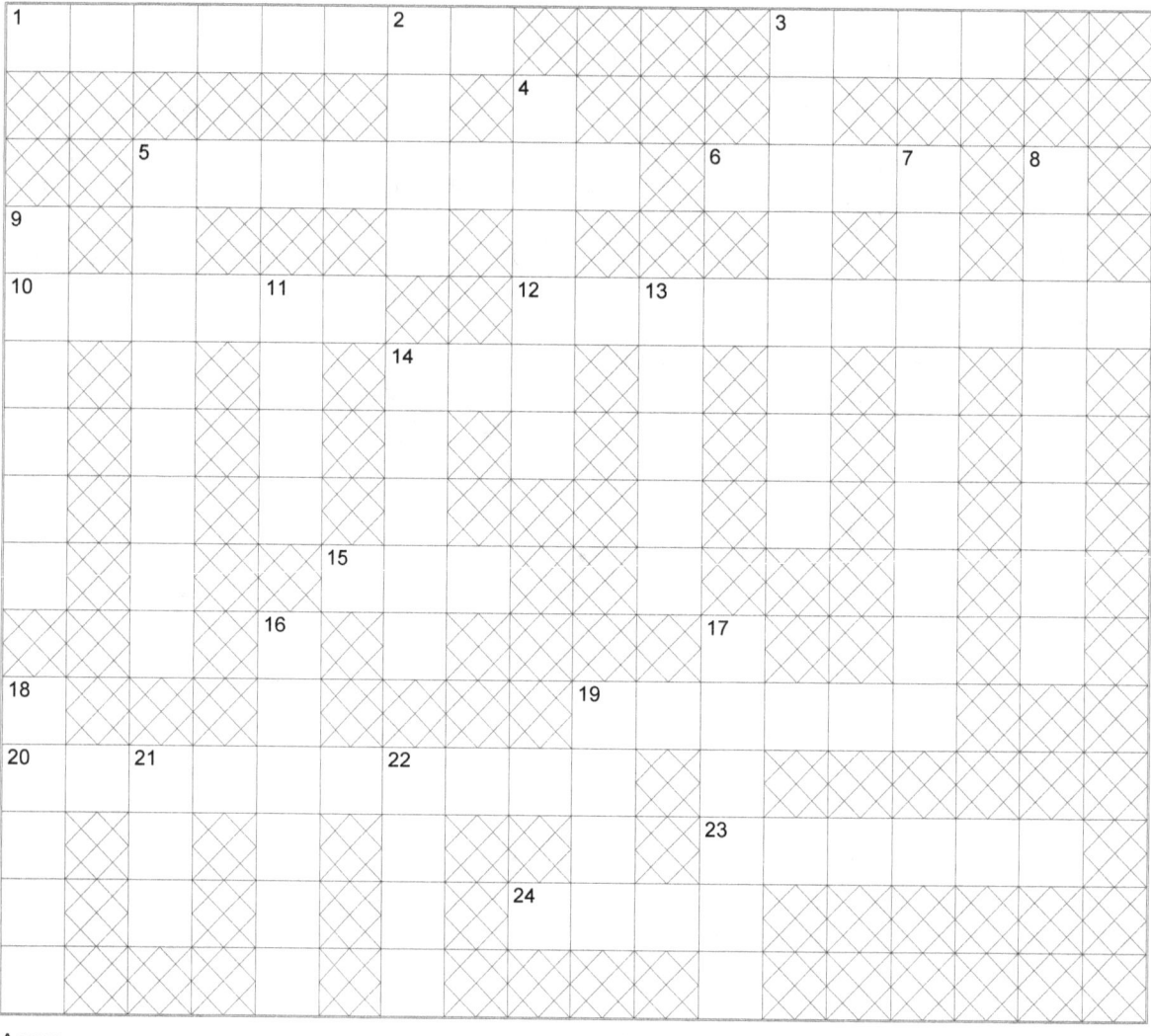

Across
1. Family's religion
3. Jeanne's older brother; led a dance-band; sent to Germany
5. ____ Homes; where the family lived after the war was over
6. Mr. Tayama's first name; he was beaten at camp and almost died
10. December 7, 1941 was the date of the Japanese _____ on Pearl Harbor
12. California city where first Japanese immigrants settled
14. Mr. Kurihara; leader of Manzanar camp riot
15. Foreman of the reservoir crew
19. Age of Jeanne's daughter when they went to the camp
20. In 1886 the Japanese government lifted its ban on _____
23. Girl ___ did not accept Jeanne as a member
24. San ____; family home for Jeanne's last year in high school

Down
2. Eleanor's husband; drafted into US Army
3. Block 16 was the location of the first ____ the family lived in
4. December 5, 1945 Manzanar camp officially _____
5. Religion to which Jeanne wanted to convert
7. Mama's job at the camp
8. Public Law 414 allowed Japanese-Americans to become US _____
9. Jeanne thought it was a misuse of the body
11. Papa's version of the samurai sword
13. Woody's wife
14. Ka-Ke; Papa's home in _____
16. Pearl ___; American base in Hawaii bombed by Japan
17. Several of Jeanne's family members moved to New ___ after the war
18. Jeanne's age when the family went to Manzanar
19. Mitsue ___ protested internment under habeas corpus & won
21. Traitor; women called Papa this
22. Bill's wife

Farewell to Manzanar Crossword 2 Answer Key

	1 B	U	D	D	H	I	2 S	T			3 B	I	L	L
							H		4 C		A			
			5 C	A	B	R	I	L	L	O		6 F	R	E	D	7		8 C
9 B		A				G		O			R		I		I
10 A	T	T	A	C	K		12 S	A	13 C	R	A	M	E	N	T	O
L		H		A		14 J	O	E		H		C		T		I
L		O		N		A		D		I		K		I		Z
E		L		E		P				Z		S		C		E
T		I		15 K	A	Z				U				I		N
		C		16 H		N				17 J				A		S
18 S				A				19 E	L	E	V	E	N
20 E	M	21 I	G	R	A	22 T	I	O	N				
V		N		B		O				23 S	C	O	U	T	S
E		U		O		M		24 J	O	S	E
N				R		I				Y

Across
1. Family's religion
3. Jeanne's older brother; led a dance-band; sent to Germany
5. ____ Homes; where the family lived after the war was over
6. Mr. Tayama's first name; he was beaten at camp and almost died
10. December 7, 1941 was the date of the Japanese _____ on Pearl Harbor
12. California city where first Japanese immigrants settled
14. Mr. Kurihara; leader of Manzanar camp riot
15. Foreman of the reservoir crew
19. Age of Jeanne's daughter when they went to the camp
20. In 1886 the Japanese government lifted its ban on _____
23. Girl ___ did not accept Jeanne as a member
24. San ____; family home for Jeanne's last year in high school

Down
2. Eleanor's husband; drafted into US Army
3. Block 16 was the location of the first ____ the family lived in
4. December 5, 1945 Manzanar camp officially _____
5. Religion to which Jeanne wanted to convert
7. Mama's job at the camp
8. Public Law 414 allowed Japanese-Americans to become US _____
9. Jeanne thought it was a misuse of the body
11. Papa's version of the samurai sword
13. Woody's wife
14. Ka-Ke; Papa's home in _____
16. Pearl ___; American base in Hawaii bombed by Japan
17. Several of Jeanne's family members moved to New ___ after the war
18. Jeanne's age when the family went to Manzanar
19. Mitsue ___ protested internment under habeas corpus & won
21. Traitor; women called Papa this
22. Bill's wife

Farewell to Manzanar Crossword 3

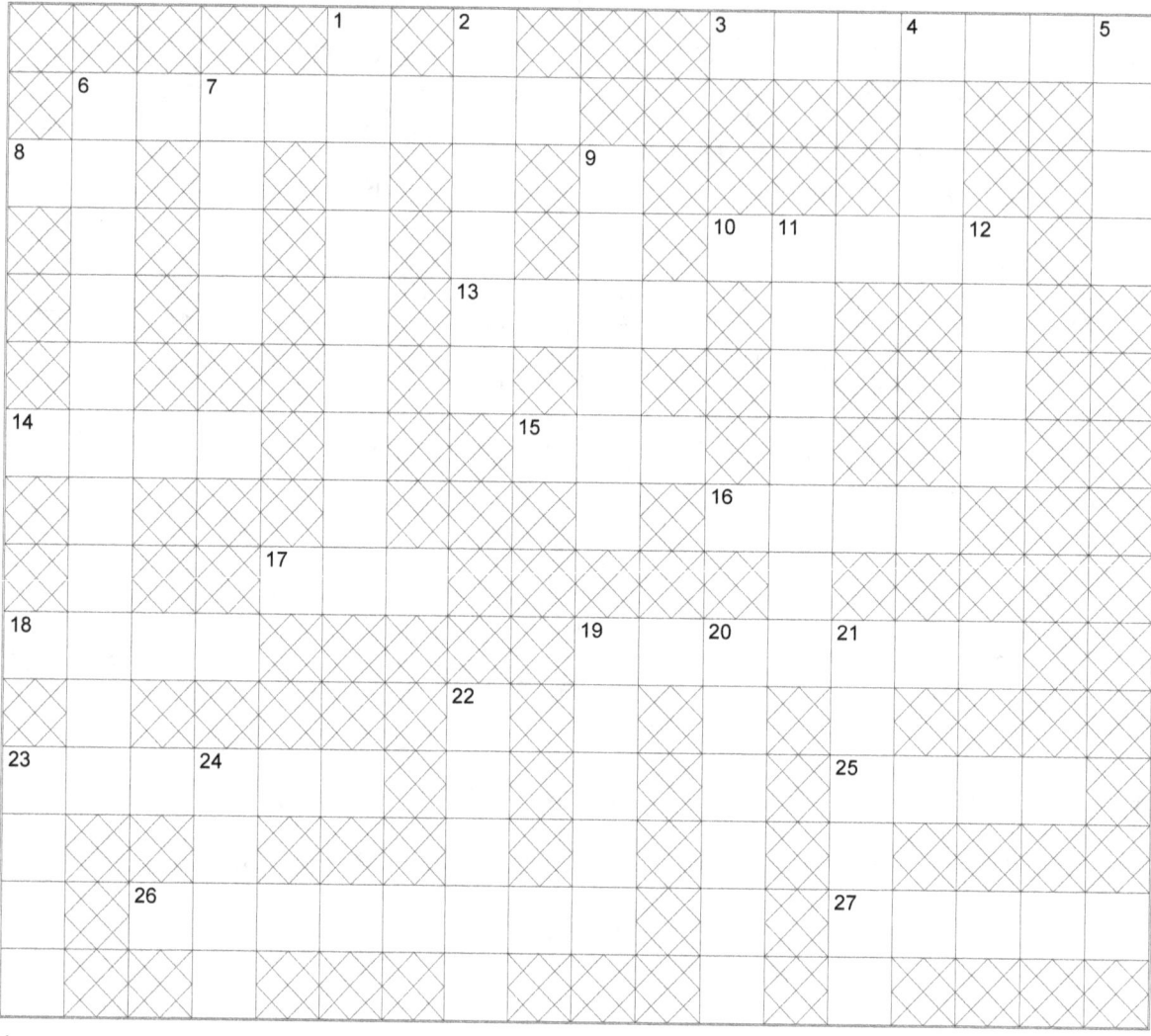

Across

3. Ft. ____; Papa was imprisoned there
6. ____ Homes; where the family lived after the war was over
8. Papa's first name
10. Jeanne's age when the family went to Manzanar
13. Mitsue ___ protested internment under habeas corpus & won
14. Mr. Tayama's first name; he was beaten at camp and almost died
15. Traitor; women called Papa this
16. Jeanne's brother; punched Papa in the face to protect Mama
17. Foreman of the reservoir crew
18. Mama worked at the ___ cannery
19. Spring of 1943 the family moved near the peach ____
23. Several of Jeanne's family members moved to New ___ after the war
25. Bill's wife
26. Public Law 414 allowed Japanese-Americans to become US _____
27. Woody's wife

Down

1. August 6, 1945 US dropped atom bomb on _____
2. Age of Jeanne's daughter when they went to the camp
4. Papa's version of the samurai sword
5. Number of months Papa spent at Ft. Lincoln
6. Papa drafted plans to start one but never started it
7. Jeanne's older brother; led a dance-band; sent to Germany
9. Jeanne's friend in junior high but not high school
11. Language Jeanne spoke
12. Model of car Papa drove out of Manzanar
19. ____ Valley, CA; location of Manzanar camp
20. 442nd ____ Regiment was an all Nisei unit in the US Army
21. December 7, 1941 was the date of the Japanese ____ on Pearl Harbor
22. Jeanne's elected position; Carnival ____
23. San ____; family home for Jeanne's last year in high school
24. Eleanor's husband; drafted into US Army

Farewell to Manzanar Crossword 3 Answer Key

				¹H		²E			³L		⁴N	C	O	L	⁵N
	⁶C	A	⁷B	R	I	L	L	O				A			I
⁸K	O		I		R	E		⁹R				N		¹²N	N
	O		L		I	V		A		¹⁰S	¹¹E	V	E	N	E
	P		L		S	¹³E	N	D	O		N			A	
	E				H	N		I			G			S	
¹⁴F	R	E	D		I	¹⁵I	N	U		¹⁶K	L	Y	O	H	
	A				M	E				I					
	T		¹⁷K	A	Z					S					
¹⁸F	I	S	H				¹⁹O	²⁰R	C	²¹H	A	R	D		
	V			²²Q		W		O		T					
²³J	E	²⁴R	S	E	Y	U		E		M	²⁵T	O	M	I	
O		S		E		N		B		A					
S	²⁶C	I	T	I	Z	E	N	S		²⁷C	H	I	Z	U	
E		G		N				T		K					

Across
3. Ft. ____; Papa was imprisoned there
6. ____ Homes; where the family lived after the war was over
8. Papa's first name
10. Jeanne's age when the family went to Manzanar
13. Mitsue ____ protested internment under habeas corpus & won
14. Mr. Tayama's first name; he was beaten at camp and almost died
15. Traitor; women called Papa this
16. Jeanne's brother; punched Papa in the face to protect Mama
17. Foreman of the reservoir crew
18. Mama worked at the ___ cannery
19. Spring of 1943 the family moved near the peach ____
23. Several of Jeanne's family members moved to New ___ after the war
25. Bill's wife
26. Public Law 414 allowed Japanese-Americans to become US _____
27. Woody's wife

Down
1. August 6, 1945 US dropped atom bomb on _____
2. Age of Jeanne's daughter when they went to the camp
4. Papa's version of the samurai sword
5. Number of months Papa spent at Ft. Lincoln
6. Papa drafted plans to start one but never started it
7. Jeanne's older brother; led a dance-band; sent to Germany
9. Jeanne's friend in junior high but not high school
11. Language Jeanne spoke
12. Model of car Papa drove out of Manzanar
19. ____ Valley, CA; location of Manzanar camp
20. 442nd ____ Regiment was an all Nisei unit in the US Army
21. December 7, 1941 was the date of the Japanese ____ on Pearl Harbor
22. Jeanne's elected position; Carnival ____
23. San ____; family home for Jeanne's last year in high school
24. Eleanor's husband; drafted into US Army

Farewell to Manzanar Crossword 4

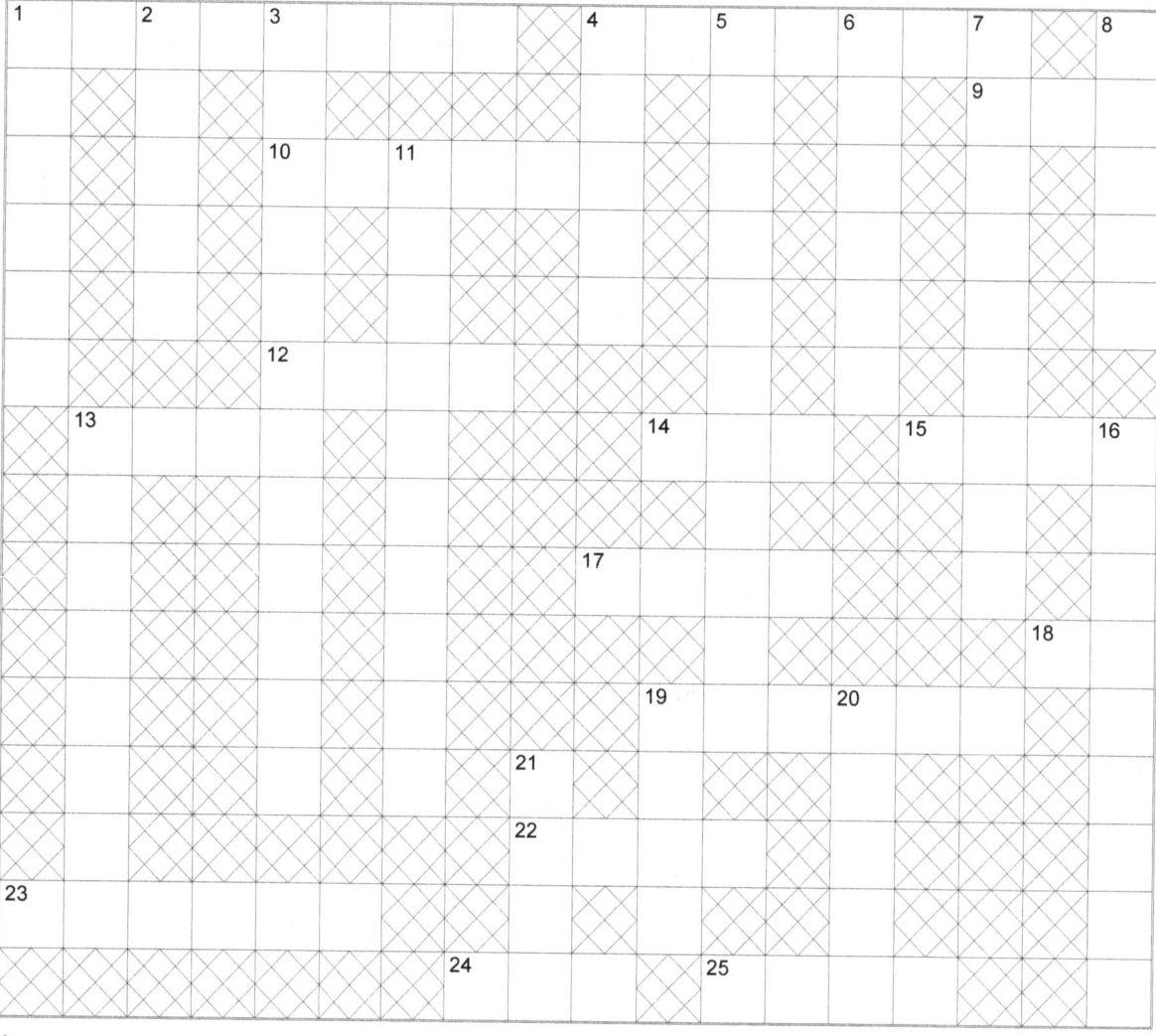

Across
1. Number of interned Japanese-Americans: 110 _____
4. Spring of 1943 the family moved near the peach _____
9. Traitor; women called Papa this
10. Jeanne's friend in junior high but not high school
12. Jeanne's older brother; led a dance-band; sent to Germany
13. Papa's version of the samurai sword
14. Foreman of the reservoir crew
15. Mama worked at the ___ cannery
17. Eleanor's husband; drafted into US Army
18. Papa's first name
19. Several of Jeanne's family members moved to New ___ after the war
22. Model of car Papa drove out of Manzanar
23. 442nd _____ Regiment was an all Nisei unit in the US Army
24. Mr. Kurihara; leader of Manzanar camp riot
25. Number of months Papa spent at Ft. Lincoln

Down
1. Number of years it took Jeanne to go back to Manzanar
2. ____ Park; where Wakatsuki family lived before their internment
3. In 1952 the family moved to San Jose and Papa raised _____
4. ____ Valley, CA; location of Manzanar camp
5. Papa drafted plans to start one but never started it
6. December 7, 1941 was the date of the Japanese _____ on Pearl Harbor
7. Mama's job at the camp
8. Jeanne's elected position; Carnival _____
11. Greatest possible disgrace for a Japanese man to be charged with
13. ____ Homes; where the family lived after the war was over
16. August 6, 1945 US dropped atom bomb on _____
19. San ____; family home for Jeanne's last year in high school
20. Jeanne's age when the family went to Manzanar
21. Mitsue ___ protested internment under habeas corpus & won

Farewell to Manzanar Crossword 4 Answer Key

	1 T	2 H	3 O	U	S	A	N	D		4 O	5 R	6 C	H	A	R	7 D	8 Q
	H	C	U							W	O	T				9 I	N	U
	I	E	T	10 R	11 A	D	I	N	E	N	O	T				E		E
	R	A	A	A	I					N	P	A				T		E
	T	N	N	W	S					S	E	C				I		N
	Y			12 B	I	L	L				R	K				C		
		13 C	A	N	E		O			14 K	A	Z		15 F	I	S	16 H
		A		R			Y					T				A		I
		B		R			A		17 S	H	I	G				N		R
		R		I			L					V				18 K		O
		I		E			T		19 J	E	R	20 S	E	Y		S
		L		S			Y		21 E		O		E				H
		L							22 N	A	S	H		V			I
23 C	O	M	B	A	T				D		E			E			M
								24 J	O	E		25 N	I	N	E		A

Across
1. Number of interned Japanese-Americans: 110 _____
4. Spring of 1943 the family moved near the peach _____
9. Traitor; women called Papa this
10. Jeanne's friend in junior high but not high school
12. Jeanne's older brother; led a dance-band; sent to Germany
13. Papa's version of the samurai sword
14. Foreman of the reservoir crew
15. Mama worked at the ___ cannery
17. Eleanor's husband; drafted into US Army
18. Papa's first name
19. Several of Jeanne's family members moved to New ___ after the war
22. Model of car Papa drove out of Manzanar
23. 442nd ____ Regiment was an all Nisei unit in the US Army
24. Mr. Kurihara; leader of Manzanar camp riot
25. Number of months Papa spent at Ft. Lincoln

Down
1. Number of years it took Jeanne to go back to Manzanar
2. ____ Park; where Wakatsuki family lived before their internment
3. In 1952 the family moved to San Jose and Papa raised _____
4. ____ Valley, CA; location of Manzanar camp
5. Papa drafted plans to start one but never started it
6. December 7, 1941 was the date of the Japanese _____ on Pearl Harbor
7. Mama's job at the camp
8. Jeanne's elected position; Carnival _____
11. Greatest possible disgrace for a Japanese man to be charged with
13. ____ Homes; where the family lived after the war was over
16. August 6, 1945 US dropped atom bomb on _____
19. San ____; family home for Jeanne's last year in high school
20. Jeanne's age when the family went to Manzanar
21. Mitsue ___ protested internment under habeas corpus & won

Farewell to Manzanar

JOSE	ATTACK	EVACUATION	CANE	BALLET
SACRAMENTO	THIRTY	INU	INTERVIEWER	QUEEN
ENGLISH	TOMI	FREE SPACE	SHIG	FISH
MANZANAR	CLOSED	COOPERATIVE	CITIZENS	KO
HIROSHIMA	NASH	ELEANOR	TERMINAL	OWENS

Farewell to Manzanar

INLAND	JERSEY	KIYO	WOODY	NINE
JOE	EMIGRATION	SCOUTS	RADINE	CHIZU
BARRACKS	SURRENDER	FREE SPACE	ENDO	BILL
BUDDHIST	KAZ	STRAWBERRIES	DIETICIAN	CABRILLO
EXCLUDE	LINCOLN	LOYALTY	FRED	SEVEN

Farewell to Manzanar

FISHERMAN	ELEANOR	INLAND	BILL	EXCLUDE
KIYO	CONGRESS	LINCOLN	BUDDHIST	ENGLISH
ENDO	LOYALTY	FREE SPACE	HIROSHIMA	EMIGRATION
FAMILY	EVACUATION	SURRENDER	BALLET	DISLOYALTY
SEVEN	INTERVIEWER	JAPAN	JERSEY	JOSE

Farewell to Manzanar

OCEAN	COMBAT	OWENS	THIRTY	NINE
ELEVEN	SCOUTS	HARBOR	INU	NASH
COOPERATIVE	FISH	FREE SPACE	THOUSAND	TERMINAL
BARRACKS	DIETICIAN	ATTACK	KAZ	TOMI
CHIZU	CABRILLO	CITIZENS	IMMIGRANTS	MANZANAR

Farewell to Manzanar

ATTACK	TERMINAL	QUEEN	CATHOLIC	FRED
THIRTY	TOMI	FISH	EMIGRATION	BALLET
SEVEN	KIYO	FREE SPACE	MANZANAR	COOPERATIVE
INTERVIEWER	DIETICIAN	INLAND	JOSE	NASH
CHIZU	INU	ELEVEN	BUDDHIST	CONGRESS

Farewell to Manzanar

LINCOLN	ELEANOR	EXCLUDE	BARRACKS	OWENS
FAMILY	EVACUATION	FISHERMAN	BILL	JAPAN
NINE	STRAWBERRIES	FREE SPACE	SHIG	ORCHARD
IMMIGRANTS	HIROSHIMA	SURRENDER	CANE	CITIZENS
JOE	ENDO	CLOSED	KO	KAZ

Farewell to Manzanar

SHIG	INLAND	DIETICIAN	DISLOYALTY	IMMIGRANTS
OWENS	HIROSHIMA	CANE	JERSEY	TERMINAL
BILL	KAZ	FREE SPACE	ENGLISH	STRAWBERRIES
TOMI	ORCHARD	CONGRESS	INU	FISH
LINCOLN	LOYALTY	KO	BARRACKS	NINE

Farewell to Manzanar

WOODY	ATTACK	OCEAN	FISHERMAN	CATHOLIC
BUDDHIST	ELEVEN	NASH	COOPERATIVE	MANZANAR
FAMILY	INTERVIEWER	FREE SPACE	SACRAMENTO	THOUSAND
CLOSED	SEVEN	CITIZENS	ENDO	EMIGRATION
ELEANOR	SURRENDER	RADINE	THIRTY	QUEEN

Farewell to Manzanar

SEVEN	TOMI	KIYO	SHIG	CATHOLIC
INLAND	FRED	OWENS	ELEVEN	WOODY
BARRACKS	THIRTY	FREE SPACE	CHIZU	ELEANOR
FISHERMAN	LOYALTY	HIROSHIMA	ATTACK	NINE
EVACUATION	CONGRESS	IMMIGRANTS	SCOUTS	THOUSAND

Farewell to Manzanar

KAZ	BILL	HARBOR	MANZANAR	CANE
CLOSED	NASH	LINCOLN	DIETICIAN	FAMILY
EXCLUDE	JOSE	FREE SPACE	JAPAN	DISLOYALTY
CABRILLO	OCEAN	COMBAT	BUDDHIST	INTERVIEWER
STRAWBERRIES	BALLET	FISH	RADINE	SURRENDER

Farewell to Manzanar

CLOSED	COMBAT	CONGRESS	DISLOYALTY	EMIGRATION
JAPAN	CABRILLO	KO	LINCOLN	EVACUATION
BUDDHIST	ENGLISH	FREE SPACE	INLAND	RADINE
DIETICIAN	COOPERATIVE	BARRACKS	HIROSHIMA	JERSEY
SEVEN	KIYO	THOUSAND	OCEAN	INTERVIEWER

Farewell to Manzanar

LOYALTY	CHIZU	WOODY	MANZANAR	CATHOLIC
STRAWBERRIES	BALLET	JOSE	NINE	ELEANOR
HARBOR	ORCHARD	FREE SPACE	CANE	CITIZENS
INU	QUEEN	THIRTY	IMMIGRANTS	SCOUTS
FISH	JOE	EXCLUDE	FISHERMAN	FRED

Farewell to Manzanar

IMMIGRANTS	SEVEN	SACRAMENTO	LINCOLN	MANZANAR
TOMI	RADINE	CHIZU	THOUSAND	FISH
BALLET	HIROSHIMA	FREE SPACE	NASH	FAMILY
BILL	TERMINAL	INTERVIEWER	ENDO	ATTACK
OWENS	SCOUTS	THIRTY	INLAND	EVACUATION

Farewell to Manzanar

BUDDHIST	ELEANOR	DIETICIAN	CANE	ORCHARD
SURRENDER	WOODY	COOPERATIVE	ELEVEN	JOSE
KIYO	KAZ	FREE SPACE	FISHERMAN	JOE
KO	JAPAN	SHIG	DISLOYALTY	EMIGRATION
CATHOLIC	ENGLISH	CABRILLO	STRAWBERRIES	JERSEY

Farewell to Manzanar

WOODY	JAPAN	HIROSHIMA	OCEAN	ENGLISH
FAMILY	SCOUTS	NASH	SURRENDER	FRED
INU	COMBAT	FREE SPACE	CABRILLO	HARBOR
EMIGRATION	KIYO	NINE	CLOSED	TOMI
COOPERATIVE	MANZANAR	INLAND	CANE	TERMINAL

Farewell to Manzanar

EVACUATION	CONGRESS	CITIZENS	ORCHARD	INTERVIEWER
JERSEY	FISHERMAN	LINCOLN	STRAWBERRIES	BILL
EXCLUDE	JOE	FREE SPACE	DISLOYALTY	ATTACK
BUDDHIST	FISH	LOYALTY	THOUSAND	OWENS
ENDO	RADINE	SHIG	CHIZU	CATHOLIC

Farewell to Manzanar

CABRILLO	CATHOLIC	DIETICIAN	BARRACKS	FISHERMAN
EMIGRATION	CITIZENS	KO	SACRAMENTO	BALLET
LOYALTY	HARBOR	FREE SPACE	CLOSED	ENDO
SCOUTS	DISLOYALTY	JAPAN	JERSEY	ELEVEN
SHIG	BILL	ATTACK	JOE	ENGLISH

Farewell to Manzanar

BUDDHIST	ORCHARD	EVACUATION	LINCOLN	OWENS
MANZANAR	FISH	FAMILY	COOPERATIVE	JOSE
INTERVIEWER	THIRTY	FREE SPACE	STRAWBERRIES	KAZ
THOUSAND	FRED	INLAND	OCEAN	TOMI
RADINE	KIYO	WOODY	INU	CANE

Farewell to Manzanar

BALLET	OWENS	HIROSHIMA	SHIG	ELEVEN
SACRAMENTO	ENGLISH	CONGRESS	BUDDHIST	INLAND
KIYO	IMMIGRANTS	FREE SPACE	NINE	TOMI
SEVEN	LINCOLN	EVACUATION	ENDO	SCOUTS
CABRILLO	LOYALTY	OCEAN	TERMINAL	JOE

Farewell to Manzanar

KO	CITIZENS	CANE	SURRENDER	JERSEY
NASH	INTERVIEWER	CLOSED	HARBOR	STRAWBERRIES
WOODY	ORCHARD	FREE SPACE	INU	COMBAT
MANZANAR	THOUSAND	EXCLUDE	CHIZU	FISHERMAN
DISLOYALTY	FAMILY	THIRTY	BARRACKS	JOSE

Farewell to Manzanar

DIETICIAN	RADINE	BALLET	BILL	CABRILLO
KO	ENDO	FAMILY	FISH	KIYO
CATHOLIC	SHIG	FREE SPACE	THIRTY	ELEVEN
FISHERMAN	DISLOYALTY	CLOSED	LINCOLN	OCEAN
COOPERATIVE	ELEANOR	OWENS	SACRAMENTO	CANE

Farewell to Manzanar

ENGLISH	TERMINAL	ORCHARD	NINE	CHIZU
JOE	EMIGRATION	KAZ	QUEEN	HIROSHIMA
BUDDHIST	STRAWBERRIES	FREE SPACE	INLAND	TOMI
SCOUTS	JERSEY	LOYALTY	EVACUATION	ATTACK
MANZANAR	HARBOR	WOODY	BARRACKS	EXCLUDE

Farewell to Manzanar

JERSEY	RADINE	SHIG	CHIZU	OCEAN
CABRILLO	ORCHARD	ENDO	MANZANAR	WOODY
DIETICIAN	LOYALTY	FREE SPACE	KAZ	KIYO
BARRACKS	COMBAT	NASH	INTERVIEWER	ATTACK
BUDDHIST	COOPERATIVE	SACRAMENTO	BILL	SCOUTS

Farewell to Manzanar

ELEVEN	THOUSAND	ELEANOR	KO	JOE
NINE	JOSE	FISHERMAN	CITIZENS	TERMINAL
CONGRESS	OWENS	FREE SPACE	STRAWBERRIES	EVACUATION
CLOSED	EMIGRATION	SEVEN	FAMILY	CATHOLIC
INU	QUEEN	TOMI	HARBOR	EXCLUDE

Farewell to Manzanar

SURRENDER	THOUSAND	TERMINAL	STRAWBERRIES	NINE
EXCLUDE	IMMIGRANTS	COOPERATIVE	CHIZU	FISHERMAN
HARBOR	BUDDHIST	FREE SPACE	CLOSED	JOSE
KAZ	SCOUTS	THIRTY	NASH	KO
EVACUATION	ELEVEN	RADINE	MANZANAR	EMIGRATION

Farewell to Manzanar

DISLOYALTY	OWENS	INU	CITIZENS	SEVEN
FISH	QUEEN	ORCHARD	LOYALTY	CANE
COMBAT	INLAND	FREE SPACE	SHIG	BARRACKS
WOODY	CABRILLO	ELEANOR	KIYO	SACRAMENTO
TOMI	JOE	HIROSHIMA	FRED	INTERVIEWER

Farewell to Manzanar

TOMI	RADINE	ORCHARD	NINE	MANZANAR
IMMIGRANTS	BARRACKS	COMBAT	FAMILY	ENDO
BILL	OWENS	FREE SPACE	INLAND	EMIGRATION
QUEEN	HARBOR	JOE	CANE	ATTACK
SEVEN	LINCOLN	KO	CLOSED	EXCLUDE

Farewell to Manzanar

NASH	WOODY	SACRAMENTO	STRAWBERRIES	ENGLISH
DISLOYALTY	SHIG	JAPAN	CONGRESS	BALLET
BUDDHIST	INTERVIEWER	FREE SPACE	CATHOLIC	EVACUATION
KAZ	LOYALTY	FISHERMAN	DIETICIAN	JOSE
ELEANOR	KIYO	ELEVEN	SURRENDER	COOPERATIVE

Farewell to Manzanar

DIETICIAN	OCEAN	TERMINAL	HIROSHIMA	ATTACK
OWENS	CHIZU	SCOUTS	EVACUATION	INTERVIEWER
IMMIGRANTS	COMBAT	FREE SPACE	BILL	KAZ
ELEVEN	LINCOLN	CANE	JOSE	ORCHARD
HARBOR	THOUSAND	JAPAN	CONGRESS	THIRTY

Farewell to Manzanar

ENDO	NASH	CITIZENS	EMIGRATION	CLOSED
COOPERATIVE	BARRACKS	FAMILY	ELEANOR	DISLOYALTY
INLAND	BALLET	FREE SPACE	SHIG	SACRAMENTO
JOE	KIYO	SEVEN	WOODY	KO
FISHERMAN	STRAWBERRIES	EXCLUDE	FISH	TOMI

Farewell to Manzanar

LINCOLN	HARBOR	WOODY	ENDO	TERMINAL
ORCHARD	THIRTY	KAZ	JOE	IMMIGRANTS
COOPERATIVE	SCOUTS	FREE SPACE	JOSE	SACRAMENTO
FISHERMAN	ENGLISH	STRAWBERRIES	TOMI	LOYALTY
ELEVEN	BARRACKS	NASH	COMBAT	RADINE

Farewell to Manzanar

INTERVIEWER	MANZANAR	KIYO	CANE	SEVEN
FAMILY	ELEANOR	CHIZU	INLAND	OWENS
EMIGRATION	BALLET	FREE SPACE	BUDDHIST	SHIG
CLOSED	INU	OCEAN	QUEEN	CITIZENS
DIETICIAN	FISH	CABRILLO	KO	ATTACK

Farewell to Manzanar Vocabulary Word List

No.	Word	Clue/Definition
1.	ACQUIESCENCE	Agreement without objection
2.	AFFIRMED	Declared to be true
3.	AGITATING	Stirring up public awareness and feeling
4.	ALIENS	Non-citizens living in a country
5.	ASSIMILATE	Become like the others in custom, etc.
6.	ASUNDER	In pieces or separate parts
7.	AUTHENTIC	Real; genuine
8.	BARRACKS	Large, plain buildings used for temporary housing
9.	BENEVOLENT	Kindly; charitable
10.	BIAS	Preference based on prejudice
11.	CAPITULATE	Surrender on certain conditions
12.	CAREENING	Rushing headlong with a swaying motion
13.	CHAOS	Great confusion & disorder
14.	COLLABORATOR	Someone who works with the enemy, as with an enemy in one's country
15.	CONFISCATORS	Authorities who take and keep things
16.	CONGESTION	An over-crowded condition
17.	CREDO	Beliefs
18.	CRINGE	Crouch in fear
19.	CUBICLES	Very small rooms
20.	DISPERSING	Going away in different directions
21.	DREDGE	Bring up
22.	DWINDLE	Make or become smaller or fewer
23.	EDICTS	Rules proclaimed by one in authority
24.	EMIGRATION	Resettling in another country
25.	FILIAL	Of a son or daughter
26.	FLOURISH	A showy display
27.	GOUGING	Digging; tearing out
28.	GROTESQUE	Ridiculous; absurd
29.	GUILELESS	Honest; straightforward
30.	HUNKER	Squat; sit back on one's heels
31.	IDEALIST	One who wants things to be perfect
32.	IMPACT	Forceful effect
33.	IMPERIOUSLY	In an arrogant, domineering way
34.	INCONGRUOUS	Out of place
35.	INEVITABLE	Unavoidable
36.	INTANGIBLE	Not able to be seen or touched
37.	INTERNMENT	Being forced to stay in a place
38.	ISSEI	First generation; born in Japan
39.	ISSUE	Matter or point of discussion
40.	LIVID	Extremely angry
41.	MAROONED	Left in a helpless condition
42.	METAMORPHOSIS	Change of form or structure
43.	NATURALIZATION	Admitted to citizenship
44.	NISEI	Second generation; Japanese born in US before WWII
45.	OBELISK	Tapering, four-sided structure with a pyramid-shaped top
46.	OBLIVION	Condition of being entirely forgotten
47.	OBSTINANCE	Stubbornness
48.	OMINOUS	Unfavorable; threatening
49.	OVERT	Public; not hidden
50.	PATRIARCH	Male head of family
51.	PLACATOR	Peacemaker
52.	POSTHUMOUS	Happening after one's death

Farewell to Manzanar Vocabulary Word List

No.	Word	Clue/Definition
53.	POTENCY	Power; strength
54.	PRECAUTIONS	Care taken beforehand
55.	PREMONITIONS	Warnings of what is to come
56.	PRIORITY	Coming in order of importance
57.	RESCINDED	Canceled
58.	RESERVOIR	Place where water is collected and stored
59.	RESIGNED	Accepting what comes without complaint
60.	SABOTEUR	Person who harms an enemy nation
61.	SANSEI	Third generation; Japanese born in US after WWII
62.	SEDATE	Calm; serious
63.	SPASM	Involuntary muscle contraction
64.	STANCE	Manner of standing
65.	SUBDUED	Overcome by force; conquered
66.	SURPLUS	Extra
67.	SUSTENANCE	Nourishment or support
68.	TINGE	A slight coloring
69.	TROUGH	Narrow, open container holding water
70.	TURBULENT	Violent
71.	TURMOIL	State of agitation or disturbance
72.	UNQUALIFIED	Complete; without lines or restrictions
73.	VALIDATION	Confirmation; support by facts
74.	VENTURE	Dare to go
75.	VIGIL	Watching
76.	VIGILANTE	Someone who takes the law into his own hands
77.	VOLITION	Decision or choice
78.	VULNERABILITY	Being open to attack or injury
79.	WARDING	Keeping away

Copyrighted

Farewell to Manzanar Vocabulary Fill In The Blank 1

_____ 1. Keeping away

_____ 2. Authorities who take and keep things

_____ 3. Nourishment or support

_____ 4. Someone who works with the enemy, as with an enemy in one's country

_____ 5. An over-crowded condition

_____ 6. Unfavorable; threatening

_____ 7. Public; not hidden

_____ 8. Someone who takes the law into his own hands

_____ 9. In an arrogant, domineering way

_____ 10. Confirmation; support by facts

_____ 11. Coming in order of importance

_____ 12. Stirring up public awareness and feeling

_____ 13. One who wants things to be perfect

_____ 14. Declared to be true

_____ 15. Change of form or structure

_____ 16. Become like the others in custom, etc.

_____ 17. Violent

_____ 18. Matter or point of discussion

_____ 19. Power; strength

_____ 20. Warnings of what is to come

Farewell to Manzanar Vocabulary Fill In The Blank 1 Answer Key

WARDING	1. Keeping away
CONFISCATORS	2. Authorities who take and keep things
SUSTENANCE	3. Nourishment or support
COLLABORATOR	4. Someone who works with the enemy, as with an enemy in one's country
CONGESTION	5. An over-crowded condition
OMINOUS	6. Unfavorable; threatening
OVERT	7. Public; not hidden
VIGILANTE	8. Someone who takes the law into his own hands
IMPERIOUSLY	9. In an arrogant, domineering way
VALIDATION	10. Confirmation; support by facts
PRIORITY	11. Coming in order of importance
AGITATING	12. Stirring up public awareness and feeling
IDEALIST	13. One who wants things to be perfect
AFFIRMED	14. Declared to be true
METAMORPHOSIS	15. Change of form or structure
ASSIMILATE	16. Become like the others in custom, etc.
TURBULENT	17. Violent
ISSUE	18. Matter or point of discussion
POTENCY	19. Power; strength
PREMONITIONS	20. Warnings of what is to come

Farewell to Manzanar Vocabulary Fill In The Blank 2

_____ 1. Out of place

_____ 2. Large, plain buildings used for temporary housing

_____ 3. Nourishment or support

_____ 4. Being forced to stay in a place

_____ 5. Peacemaker

_____ 6. Stirring up public awareness and feeling

_____ 7. Real; genuine

_____ 8. Complete; without lines or restrictions

_____ 9. Manner of standing

_____ 10. Non-citizens living in a country

_____ 11. Extra

_____ 12. Honest; straightforward

_____ 13. Kindly; charitable

_____ 14. Narrow, open container holding water

_____ 15. Condition of being entirely forgotten

_____ 16. Left in a helpless condition

_____ 17. Public; not hidden

_____ 18. Forceful effect

_____ 19. A showy display

_____ 20. Happening after one's death

Farewell to Manzanar Vocabulary Fill In The Blank 2 Answer Key

INCONGRUOUS	1. Out of place
BARRACKS	2. Large, plain buildings used for temporary housing
SUSTENANCE	3. Nourishment or support
INTERNMENT	4. Being forced to stay in a place
PLACATOR	5. Peacemaker
AGITATING	6. Stirring up public awareness and feeling
AUTHENTIC	7. Real; genuine
UNQUALIFIED	8. Complete; without lines or restrictions
STANCE	9. Manner of standing
ALIENS	10. Non-citizens living in a country
SURPLUS	11. Extra
GUILELESS	12. Honest; straightforward
BENEVOLENT	13. Kindly; charitable
TROUGH	14. Narrow, open container holding water
OBLIVION	15. Condition of being entirely forgotten
MAROONED	16. Left in a helpless condition
OVERT	17. Public; not hidden
IMPACT	18. Forceful effect
FLOURISH	19. A showy display
POSTHUMOUS	20. Happening after one's death

Farewell to Manzanar Vocabulary Fill In The Blank 3

_____ 1. Preference based on prejudice

_____ 2. Keeping away

_____ 3. Digging; tearing out

_____ 4. Third generation; Japanese born in US after WWII

_____ 5. An over-crowded condition

_____ 6. Unfavorable; threatening

_____ 7. One who wants things to be perfect

_____ 8. Real; genuine

_____ 9. Person who harms an enemy nation

_____ 10. Resettling in another country

_____ 11. Someone who works with the enemy, as with an enemy in one's country

_____ 12. Male head of family

_____ 13. A showy display

_____ 14. Stubbornness

_____ 15. Beliefs

_____ 16. Honest; straightforward

_____ 17. Matter or point of discussion

_____ 18. Become like the others in custom, etc.

_____ 19. Overcome by force; conquered

_____ 20. Ridiculous; absurd

Farewell to Manzanar Vocabulary Fill In The Blank 3 Answer Key

BIAS	1. Preference based on prejudice
WARDING	2. Keeping away
GOUGING	3. Digging; tearing out
SANSEI	4. Third generation; Japanese born in US after WWII
CONGESTION	5. An over-crowded condition
OMINOUS	6. Unfavorable; threatening
IDEALIST	7. One who wants things to be perfect
AUTHENTIC	8. Real; genuine
SABOTEUR	9. Person who harms an enemy nation
EMIGRATION	10. Resettling in another country
COLLABORATOR	11. Someone who works with the enemy, as with an enemy in one's country
PATRIARCH	12. Male head of family
FLOURISH	13. A showy display
OBSTINANCE	14. Stubbornness
CREDO	15. Beliefs
GUILELESS	16. Honest; straightforward
ISSUE	17. Matter or point of discussion
ASSIMILATE	18. Become like the others in custom, etc.
SUBDUED	19. Overcome by force; conquered
GROTESQUE	20. Ridiculous; absurd

Farewell to Manzanar Vocabulary Fill In The Blank 4

_____ 1. Keeping away

_____ 2. Declared to be true

_____ 3. Complete; without lines or restrictions

_____ 4. Left in a helpless condition

_____ 5. Unfavorable; threatening

_____ 6. Forceful effect

_____ 7. Condition of being entirely forgotten

_____ 8. Person who harms an enemy nation

_____ 9. Watching

_____ 10. Going away in different directions

_____ 11. Extremely angry

_____ 12. Accepting what comes without complaint

_____ 13. Someone who works with the enemy, as with an enemy in one's country

_____ 14. Unavoidable

_____ 15. Out of place

_____ 16. A showy display

_____ 17. Extra

_____ 18. In pieces or separate parts

_____ 19. Power; strength

_____ 20. Admitted to citizenship

Farewell to Manzanar Vocabulary Fill In The Blank 4 Answer Key

WARDING	1. Keeping away
AFFIRMED	2. Declared to be true
UNQUALIFIED	3. Complete; without lines or restrictions
MAROONED	4. Left in a helpless condition
OMINOUS	5. Unfavorable; threatening
IMPACT	6. Forceful effect
OBLIVION	7. Condition of being entirely forgotten
SABOTEUR	8. Person who harms an enemy nation
VIGIL	9. Watching
DISPERSING	10. Going away in different directions
LIVID	11. Extremely angry
RESIGNED	12. Accepting what comes without complaint
COLLABORATOR	13. Someone who works with the enemy, as with an enemy in one's country
INEVITABLE	14. Unavoidable
INCONGRUOUS	15. Out of place
FLOURISH	16. A showy display
SURPLUS	17. Extra
ASUNDER	18. In pieces or separate parts
POTENCY	19. Power; strength
NATURALIZATION	20. Admitted to citizenship

Farewell to Manzanar Vocabulary Matching 1

___ 1. PREMONITIONS   A. Ridiculous; absurd
___ 2. AGITATING   B. Not able to be seen or touched
___ 3. GROTESQUE   C. Watching
___ 4. INTANGIBLE   D. Rushing headlong with a swaying motion
___ 5. FILIAL   E. Preference based on prejudice
___ 6. SPASM   F. Happening after one's death
___ 7. CRINGE   G. Third generation; Japanese born in US after WWII
___ 8. PLACATOR   H. Peacemaker
___ 9. BIAS   I. Agreement without objection
___10. POSTHUMOUS   J. Tapering, four-sided structure with a pyramid-shaped top
___11. SANSEI   K. Of a son or daughter
___12. VALIDATION   L. Stirring up public awareness and feeling
___13. BENEVOLENT   M. Accepting what comes without complaint
___14. ACQUIESCENCE   N. Involuntary muscle contraction
___15. RESERVOIR   O. Honest; straightforward
___16. VENTURE   P. Manner of standing
___17. VULNERABILITY   Q. Authorities who take and keep things
___18. GUILELESS   R. Crouch in fear
___19. OBELISK   S. Beliefs
___20. CAREENING   T. Warnings of what is to come
___21. VIGIL   U. Dare to go
___22. STANCE   V. Confirmation; support by facts
___23. RESIGNED   W. Kindly; charitable
___24. CONFISCATORS   X. Being open to attack or injury
___25. CREDO   Y. Place where water is collected and stored

Farewell to Manzanar Vocabulary Matching 1 Answer Key

T - 1. PREMONITIONS	A. Ridiculous; absurd
L - 2. AGITATING	B. Not able to be seen or touched
A - 3. GROTESQUE	C. Watching
B - 4. INTANGIBLE	D. Rushing headlong with a swaying motion
K - 5. FILIAL	E. Preference based on prejudice
N - 6. SPASM	F. Happening after one's death
R - 7. CRINGE	G. Third generation; Japanese born in US after WWII
H - 8. PLACATOR	H. Peacemaker
E - 9. BIAS	I. Agreement without objection
F - 10. POSTHUMOUS	J. Tapering, four-sided structure with a pyramid-shaped top
G - 11. SANSEI	K. Of a son or daughter
V - 12. VALIDATION	L. Stirring up public awareness and feeling
W - 13. BENEVOLENT	M. Accepting what comes without complaint
I - 14. ACQUIESCENCE	N. Involuntary muscle contraction
Y - 15. RESERVOIR	O. Honest; straightforward
U - 16. VENTURE	P. Manner of standing
X - 17. VULNERABILITY	Q. Authorities who take and keep things
O - 18. GUILELESS	R. Crouch in fear
J - 19. OBELISK	S. Beliefs
D - 20. CAREENING	T. Warnings of what is to come
C - 21. VIGIL	U. Dare to go
P - 22. STANCE	V. Confirmation; support by facts
M - 23. RESIGNED	W. Kindly; charitable
Q - 24. CONFISCATORS	X. Being open to attack or injury
S - 25. CREDO	Y. Place where water is collected and stored

Farewell to Manzanar Vocabulary Matching 2

___ 1. SABOTEUR   A. State of agitation or disturbance
___ 2. GROTESQUE   B. Matter or point of discussion
___ 3. AUTHENTIC   C. Make or become smaller or fewer
___ 4. TROUGH   D. Bring up
___ 5. VIGILANTE   E. Preference based on prejudice
___ 6. IDEALIST   F. Person who harms an enemy nation
___ 7. NISEI   G. Being forced to stay in a place
___ 8. PATRIARCH   H. Nourishment or support
___ 9. BIAS   I. Unfavorable; threatening
___ 10. EDICTS   J. Change of form or structure
___ 11. MAROONED   K. Ridiculous; absurd
___ 12. INTERNMENT   L. Keeping away
___ 13. METAMORPHOSIS   M. An over-crowded condition
___ 14. DWINDLE   N. Rules proclaimed by one in authority
___ 15. ISSEI   O. One who wants things to be perfect
___ 16. CONGESTION   P. Someone who takes the law into his own hands
___ 17. SUSTENANCE   Q. In an arrogant, domineering way
___ 18. OMINOUS   R. Second generation; Japanese born in US before WWII
___ 19. TURMOIL   S. Involuntary muscle contraction
___ 20. WARDING   T. Narrow, open container holding water
___ 21. LIVID   U. Male head of family
___ 22. IMPERIOUSLY   V. Left in a helpless condition
___ 23. SPASM   W. Real; genuine
___ 24. ISSUE   X. First generation; born in Japan
___ 25. DREDGE   Y. Extremely angry

Farewell to Manzanar Vocabulary Matching 2 Answer Key

F - 1. SABOTEUR		A. State of agitation or disturbance
K - 2. GROTESQUE		B. Matter or point of discussion
W - 3. AUTHENTIC		C. Make or become smaller or fewer
T - 4. TROUGH		D. Bring up
P - 5. VIGILANTE		E. Preference based on prejudice
O - 6. IDEALIST		F. Person who harms an enemy nation
R - 7. NISEI		G. Being forced to stay in a place
U - 8. PATRIARCH		H. Nourishment or support
E - 9. BIAS		I. Unfavorable; threatening
N -10. EDICTS		J. Change of form or structure
V -11. MAROONED		K. Ridiculous; absurd
G -12. INTERNMENT		L. Keeping away
J -13. METAMORPHOSIS		M. An over-crowded condition
C -14. DWINDLE		N. Rules proclaimed by one in authority
X -15. ISSEI		O. One who wants things to be perfect
M -16. CONGESTION		P. Someone who takes the law into his own hands
H -17. SUSTENANCE		Q. In an arrogant, domineering way
I -18. OMINOUS		R. Second generation; Japanese born in US before WWII
A -19. TURMOIL		S. Involuntary muscle contraction
L -20. WARDING		T. Narrow, open container holding water
Y -21. LIVID		U. Male head of family
Q -22. IMPERIOUSLY		V. Left in a helpless condition
S -23. SPASM		W. Real; genuine
B -24. ISSUE		X. First generation; born in Japan
D -25. DREDGE		Y. Extremely angry

Farewell to Manzanar Vocabulary Matching 3

___ 1. INCONGRUOUS   A. Public; not hidden
___ 2. TURBULENT   B. Admitted to citizenship
___ 3. VENTURE   C. Peacemaker
___ 4. ASUNDER   D. Power; strength
___ 5. PLACATOR   E. State of agitation or disturbance
___ 6. GROTESQUE   F. Stirring up public awareness and feeling
___ 7. POTENCY   G. Nourishment or support
___ 8. GOUGING   H. Out of place
___ 9. RESERVOIR   I. Dare to go
___10. VULNERABILITY   J. Digging; tearing out
___11. SUBDUED   K. Place where water is collected and stored
___12. PATRIARCH   L. Being open to attack or injury
___13. OBLIVION   M. Authorities who take and keep things
___14. CAREENING   N. Overcome by force; conquered
___15. CONFISCATORS   O. Condition of being entirely forgotten
___16. OVERT   P. Rushing headlong with a swaying motion
___17. EMIGRATION   Q. Make or become smaller or fewer
___18. SUSTENANCE   R. Declared to be true
___19. AFFIRMED   S. In pieces or separate parts
___20. TINGE   T. Male head of family
___21. ALIENS   U. Non-citizens living in a country
___22. NATURALIZATION   V. Resettling in another country
___23. DWINDLE   W. Ridiculous; absurd
___24. TURMOIL   X. Violent
___25. AGITATING   Y. A slight coloring

Farewell to Manzanar Vocabulary Matching 3 Answer Key

H - 1. INCONGRUOUS	A.	Public; not hidden
X - 2. TURBULENT	B.	Admitted to citizenship
I - 3. VENTURE	C.	Peacemaker
S - 4. ASUNDER	D.	Power; strength
C - 5. PLACATOR	E.	State of agitation or disturbance
W - 6. GROTESQUE	F.	Stirring up public awareness and feeling
D - 7. POTENCY	G.	Nourishment or support
J - 8. GOUGING	H.	Out of place
K - 9. RESERVOIR	I.	Dare to go
L - 10. VULNERABILITY	J.	Digging; tearing out
N - 11. SUBDUED	K.	Place where water is collected and stored
T - 12. PATRIARCH	L.	Being open to attack or injury
O - 13. OBLIVION	M.	Authorities who take and keep things
P - 14. CAREENING	N.	Overcome by force; conquered
M - 15. CONFISCATORS	O.	Condition of being entirely forgotten
A - 16. OVERT	P.	Rushing headlong with a swaying motion
V - 17. EMIGRATION	Q.	Make or become smaller or fewer
G - 18. SUSTENANCE	R.	Declared to be true
R - 19. AFFIRMED	S.	In pieces or separate parts
Y - 20. TINGE	T.	Male head of family
U - 21. ALIENS	U.	Non-citizens living in a country
B - 22. NATURALIZATION	V.	Resettling in another country
Q - 23. DWINDLE	W.	Ridiculous; absurd
E - 24. TURMOIL	X.	Violent
F - 25. AGITATING	Y.	A slight coloring

Farewell to Manzanar Vocabulary Matching 4

___ 1. VIGIL   A. Warnings of what is to come
___ 2. RESIGNED   B. Ridiculous; absurd
___ 3. GROTESQUE   C. Resettling in another country
___ 4. VALIDATION   D. Stirring up public awareness and feeling
___ 5. EMIGRATION   E. Watching
___ 6. PRIORITY   F. Keeping away
___ 7. TURMOIL   G. Left in a helpless condition
___ 8. PREMONITIONS   H. Peacemaker
___ 9. VULNERABILITY   I. Care taken beforehand
___10. PLACATOR   J. Being open to attack or injury
___11. WARDING   K. State of agitation or disturbance
___12. METAMORPHOSIS   L. In pieces or separate parts
___13. AGITATING   M. Confirmation; support by facts
___14. SANSEI   N. Third generation; Japanese born in US after WWII
___15. MAROONED   O. Very small rooms
___16. ASUNDER   P. Coming in order of importance
___17. CUBICLES   Q. Decision or choice
___18. SUBDUED   R. Accepting what comes without complaint
___19. RESERVOIR   S. Place where water is collected and stored
___20. PRECAUTIONS   T. Overcome by force; conquered
___21. PATRIARCH   U. Non-citizens living in a country
___22. ISSEI   V. Male head of family
___23. ALIENS   W. Declared to be true
___24. VOLITION   X. Change of form or structure
___25. AFFIRMED   Y. First generation; born in Japan

Farewell to Manzanar Vocabulary Matching 4 Answer Key

E - 1.	VIGIL	A. Warnings of what is to come
R - 2.	RESIGNED	B. Ridiculous; absurd
B - 3.	GROTESQUE	C. Resettling in another country
M - 4.	VALIDATION	D. Stirring up public awareness and feeling
C - 5.	EMIGRATION	E. Watching
P - 6.	PRIORITY	F. Keeping away
K - 7.	TURMOIL	G. Left in a helpless condition
A - 8.	PREMONITIONS	H. Peacemaker
J - 9.	VULNERABILITY	I. Care taken beforehand
H - 10.	PLACATOR	J. Being open to attack or injury
F - 11.	WARDING	K. State of agitation or disturbance
X - 12.	METAMORPHOSIS	L. In pieces or separate parts
D - 13.	AGITATING	M. Confirmation; support by facts
N - 14.	SANSEI	N. Third generation; Japanese born in US after WWII
G - 15.	MAROONED	O. Very small rooms
L - 16.	ASUNDER	P. Coming in order of importance
O - 17.	CUBICLES	Q. Decision or choice
T - 18.	SUBDUED	R. Accepting what comes without complaint
S - 19.	RESERVOIR	S. Place where water is collected and stored
I - 20.	PRECAUTIONS	T. Overcome by force; conquered
V - 21.	PATRIARCH	U. Non-citizens living in a country
Y - 22.	ISSEI	V. Male head of family
U - 23.	ALIENS	W. Declared to be true
Q - 24.	VOLITION	X. Change of form or structure
W - 25.	AFFIRMED	Y. First generation; born in Japan

Farewell to Manzanar Vocabulary Magic Squares 1

Match the definition with the vocabulary word. Put your answers in the magic squares below. When your answers are correct, all columns and rows will add to the same number.

A. OBELISK
B. PLACATOR
C. TURBULENT
D. IDEALIST
E. TROUGH
F. NATURALIZATION
G. DREDGE
H. CUBICLES
I. ISSEI
J. FILIAL
K. OMINOUS
L. INEVITABLE
M. TURMOIL
N. METAMORPHOSIS
O. PRECAUTIONS
P. SPASM

1. Tapering, four-sided structure with a pyramid-shaped top
2. Change of form or structure
3. Of a son or daughter
4. Narrow, open container holding water
5. Bring up
6. Unavoidable
7. Involuntary muscle contraction
8. Violent
9. Care taken beforehand
10. One who wants things to be perfect
11. Very small rooms
12. Unfavorable; threatening
13. First generation; born in Japan
14. Admitted to citizenship
15. Peacemaker
16. State of agitation or disturbance

A=	B=	C=	D=
E=	F=	G=	H=
I=	J=	K=	L=
M=	N=	O=	P=

Farewell to Manzanar Vocabulary Magic Squares 1 Answer Key

Match the definition with the vocabulary word. Put your answers in the magic squares below. When your answers are correct, all columns and rows will add to the same number.

A. OBELISK
B. PLACATOR
C. TURBULENT
D. IDEALIST
E. TROUGH
F. NATURALIZATION
G. DREDGE
H. CUBICLES
I. ISSEI
J. FILIAL
K. OMINOUS
L. INEVITABLE
M. TURMOIL
N. METAMORPHOSIS
O. PRECAUTIONS
P. SPASM

1. Tapering, four-sided structure with a pyramid-shaped top
2. Change of form or structure
3. Of a son or daughter
4. Narrow, open container holding water
5. Bring up
6. Unavoidable
7. Involuntary muscle contraction
8. Violent
9. Care taken beforehand
10. One who wants things to be perfect
11. Very small rooms
12. Unfavorable; threatening
13. First generation; born in Japan
14. Admitted to citizenship
15. Peacemaker
16. State of agitation or disturbance

A=1	B=15	C=8	D=10
E=4	F=14	G=5	H=11
I=13	J=3	K=12	L=6
M=16	N=2	O=9	P=7

Farewell to Manzanar Vocabulary Magic Squares 2

Match the definition with the vocabulary word. Put your answers in the magic squares below. When your answers are correct, all columns and rows will add to the same number.

A. TINGE
B. AGITATING
C. NISEI
D. ASSIMILATE
E. CUBICLES
F. SURPLUS
G. SUBDUED
H. OVERT
I. LIVID
J. GOUGING
K. DWINDLE
L. AFFIRMED
M. SEDATE
N. TURBULENT
O. OBSTINANCE
P. COLLABORATOR

1. Stubbornness
2. Become like the others in custom, etc.
3. Digging; tearing out
4. Very small rooms
5. Extremely angry
6. Extra
7. Someone who works with the enemy, as with an enemy in one's country
8. Second generation; Japanese born in US before WWII
9. Public; not hidden
10. Make or become smaller or fewer
11. A slight coloring
12. Violent
13. Stirring up public awareness and feeling
14. Calm; serious
15. Overcome by force; conquered
16. Declared to be true

A=	B=	C=	D=
E=	F=	G=	H=
I=	J=	K=	L=
M=	N=	O=	P=

Farewell to Manzanar Vocabulary Magic Squares 2 Answer Key

Match the definition with the vocabulary word. Put your answers in the magic squares below. When your answers are correct, all columns and rows will add to the same number.

A. TINGE
B. AGITATING
C. NISEI
D. ASSIMILATE
E. CUBICLES
F. SURPLUS
G. SUBDUED
H. OVERT
I. LIVID
J. GOUGING
K. DWINDLE
L. AFFIRMED
M. SEDATE
N. TURBULENT
O. OBSTINANCE
P. COLLABORATOR

1. Stubbornness
2. Become like the others in custom, etc.
3. Digging; tearing out
4. Very small rooms
5. Extremely angry
6. Extra
7. Someone who works with the enemy, as with an enemy in one's country
8. Second generation; Japanese born in US before WWII
9. Public; not hidden
10. Make or become smaller or fewer
11. A slight coloring
12. Violent
13. Stirring up public awareness and feeling
14. Calm; serious
15. Overcome by force; conquered
16. Declared to be true

A=11	B=13	C=8	D=2
E=4	F=6	G=15	H=9
I=5	J=3	K=10	L=16
M=14	N=12	O=1	P=7

Copyrighted

Farewell to Manzanar Vocabulary Magic Squares 3

Match the definition with the vocabulary word. Put your answers in the magic squares below. When your answers are correct, all columns and rows will add to the same number.

A. SABOTEUR
B. HUNKER
C. INTERNMENT
D. SANSEI
E. VALIDATION
F. IMPERIOUSLY
G. DISPERSING
H. ISSEI
I. ISSUE
J. COLLABORATOR
K. TINGE
L. POSTHUMOUS
M. PRECAUTIONS
N. VOLITION
O. FLOURISH
P. CAPITULATE

1. Being forced to stay in a place
2. Someone who works with the enemy, as with an enemy in one's country
3. In an arrogant, domineering way
4. A showy display
5. Surrender on certain conditions
6. Confirmation; support by facts
7. Matter or point of discussion
8. Third generation; Japanese born in US after WWII
9. Care taken beforehand
10. First generation; born in Japan
11. Happening after one's death
12. Person who harms an enemy nation
13. Squat; sit back on one's heels
14. A slight coloring
15. Going away in different directions
16. Decision or choice

A=	B=	C=	D=
E=	F=	G=	H=
I=	J=	K=	L=
M=	N=	O=	P=

Farewell to Manzanar Vocabulary Magic Squares 3 Answer Key

Match the definition with the vocabulary word. Put your answers in the magic squares below. When your answers are correct, all columns and rows will add to the same number.

A. SABOTEUR
B. HUNKER
C. INTERNMENT
D. SANSEI
E. VALIDATION
F. IMPERIOUSLY
G. DISPERSING
H. ISSEI
I. ISSUE
J. COLLABORATOR
K. TINGE
L. POSTHUMOUS
M. PRECAUTIONS
N. VOLITION
O. FLOURISH
P. CAPITULATE

1. Being forced to stay in a place
2. Someone who works with the enemy, as with an enemy in one's country
3. In an arrogant, domineering way
4. A showy display
5. Surrender on certain conditions
6. Confirmation; support by facts
7. Matter or point of discussion
8. Third generation; Japanese born in US after WWII
9. Care taken beforehand
10. First generation; born in Japan
11. Happening after one's death
12. Person who harms an enemy nation
13. Squat; sit back on one's heels
14. A slight coloring
15. Going away in different directions
16. Decision or choice

A=12	B=13	C=1	D=8
E=6	F=3	G=15	H=10
I=7	J=2	K=14	L=11
M=9	N=16	O=4	P=5

85
Copyrighted

Farewell to Manzanar Vocabulary Magic Squares 4

Match the definition with the vocabulary word. Put your answers in the magic squares below. When your answers are correct, all columns and rows will add to the same number.

A. DREDGE
B. VENTURE
C. NATURALIZATION
D. CUBICLES
E. TURBULENT
F. FILIAL
G. CONGESTION
H. COLLABORATOR
I. DWINDLE
J. EDICTS
K. OBSTINANCE
L. GUILELESS
M. INEVITABLE
N. ACQUIESCENCE
O. PRIORITY
P. POSTHUMOUS

1. Of a son or daughter
2. Make or become smaller or fewer
3. Coming in order of importance
4. Very small rooms
5. Unavoidable
6. Dare to go
7. Someone who works with the enemy, as with an enemy in one's country
8. Stubbornness
9. Admitted to citizenship
10. Happening after one's death
11. Rules proclaimed by one in authority
12. Violent
13. Honest; straightforward
14. An over-crowded condition
15. Bring up
16. Agreement without objection

A=	B=	C=	D=
E=	F=	G=	H=
I=	J=	K=	L=
M=	N=	O=	P=

Farewell to Manzanar Vocabulary Magic Squares 4 Answer Key

Match the definition with the vocabulary word. Put your answers in the magic squares below. When your answers are correct, all columns and rows will add to the same number.

A. DREDGE
B. VENTURE
C. NATURALIZATION
D. CUBICLES
E. TURBULENT
F. FILIAL
G. CONGESTION
H. COLLABORATOR
I. DWINDLE
J. EDICTS
K. OBSTINANCE
L. GUILELESS
M. INEVITABLE
N. ACQUIESCENCE
O. PRIORITY
P. POSTHUMOUS

1. Of a son or daughter
2. Make or become smaller or fewer
3. Coming in order of importance
4. Very small rooms
5. Unavoidable
6. Dare to go
7. Someone who works with the enemy, as with an enemy in one's country
8. Stubbornness
9. Admitted to citizenship
10. Happening after one's death
11. Rules proclaimed by one in authority
12. Violent
13. Honest; straightforward
14. An over-crowded condition
15. Bring up
16. Agreement without objection

A=15	B=6	C=9	D=4
E=12	F=1	G=14	H=7
I=2	J=11	K=8	L=13
M=5	N=16	O=3	P=10

Farewell to Manzanar Vocabulary Word Search 1

```
I N T E R N M E N T D I S P E R S I N G
S N F T V I G I L F R O O S C V O D T R
T A T N L L T N D E E B B U N O A C S S
C S R A L I W Q D Z D E L R A L H F R Y
I S O L N B V N Y J G L I P T I C E Q F
D I T I W G U I C V E I V L S T S B C H
E M A G G S I L D A Y S I U F I L I A L
T I C I A U I B Q Y R K O S G O Y O S K
A L A V P O I H L N Q E N N E N F V P M
L A L U M Y D L N E K W E R G D D E A L
U T P R T L B S E Y Z D Z N N E A R S T
T E U R O H P V A L I D A T I O N T M S
I T P D R P E I H K E D R F T N N S E I
P K E A C I S N M K L S I H H E G G E Z
A R B L Q W S I T P P L S G L U N S L T
C U B I C L E S X I A G O U G I N G P X
V L D E A F B E U U C C B O D A S K W F
L Y P N Z S J I Q E L R T R S Y V S E K
R M Z S C R I N G E U Y A T W M B W E R
S D E U D B U S F T L W V E N T U R E I
```

A slight coloring (5)
Accepting what comes without complaint (8)
Become like the others in custom, etc. (10)
Being forced to stay in a place (10)
Beliefs (5)
Bring up (6)
Calm; serious (6)
Complete; without lines or restrictions (11)
Condition of being entirely forgotten (8)
Confirmation; support by facts (10)
Crouch in fear (6)
Dare to go (7)
Decision or choice (8)
Digging; tearing out (7)
Extra (7)
Extremely angry (5)
First generation; born in Japan (5)
Forceful effect (6)
Going away in different directions (10)
Great confusion & disorder (5)
Honest; straightforward (9)
In pieces or separate parts (7)
Involuntary muscle contraction (5)
Keeping away (7)
Manner of standing (6)
Matter or point of discussion (5)

Narrow, open container holding water (6)
Non-citizens living in a country (6)
Not able to be seen or touched (10)
Of a son or daughter (6)
Overcome by force; conquered (7)
Peacemaker (8)
Preference based on prejudice (4)
Public; not hidden (5)
Real; genuine (9)
Rules proclaimed by one in authority (6)
Rushing headlong with a swaying motion (9)
Second generation; Japanese born in US
  before WWII (5)
Someone who takes the law into his own
  hands (9)
Squat; sit back on one's heels (6)
State of agitation or disturbance (7)
Surrender on certain conditions (10)
Tapering, four-sided structure with a
  pyramid-shaped top (7)
Third generation; Japanese born in US after
  WWII (6)
Very small rooms (8)
Violent (9)
Watching (5)

Farewell to Manzanar Vocabulary Word Search 1 Answer Key

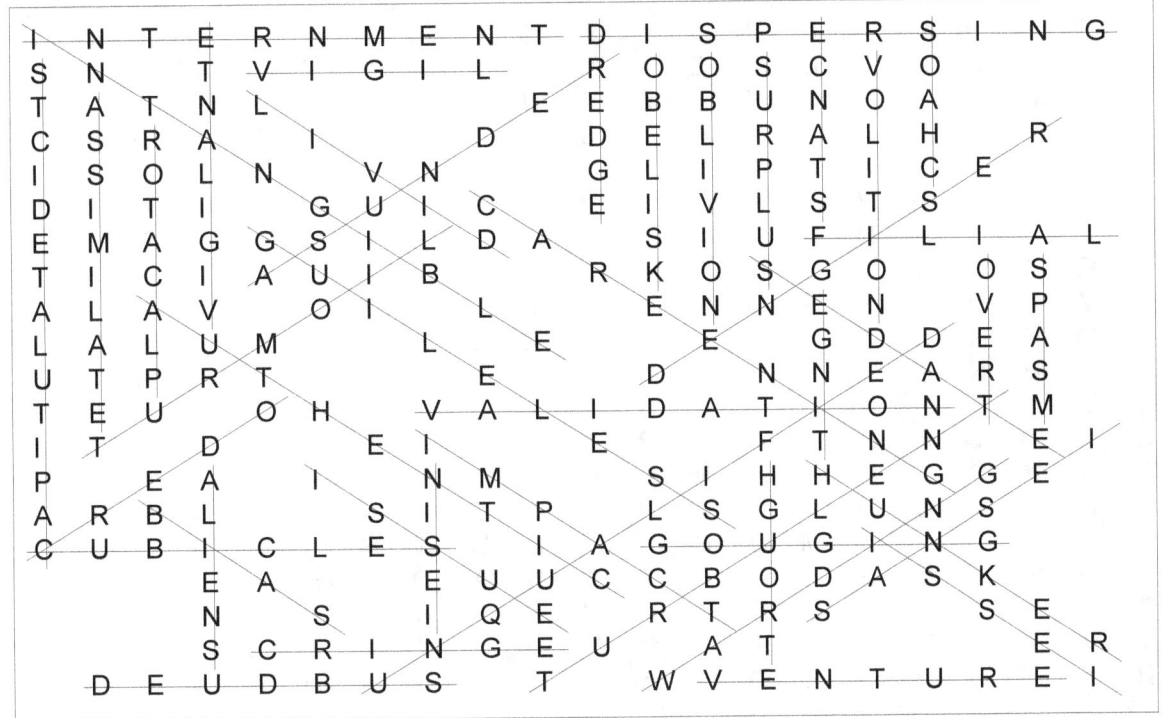

A slight coloring (5)
Accepting what comes without complaint (8)
Become like the others in custom, etc. (10)
Being forced to stay in a place (10)
Beliefs (5)
Bring up (6)
Calm; serious (6)
Complete; without lines or restrictions (11)
Condition of being entirely forgotten (8)
Confirmation; support by facts (10)
Crouch in fear (6)
Dare to go (7)
Decision or choice (8)
Digging; tearing out (7)
Extra (7)
Extremely angry (5)
First generation; born in Japan (5)
Forceful effect (6)
Going away in different directions (10)
Great confusion & disorder (5)
Honest; straightforward (9)
In pieces or separate parts (7)
Involuntary muscle contraction (5)
Keeping away (7)
Manner of standing (6)
Matter or point of discussion (5)

Narrow, open container holding water (6)
Non-citizens living in a country (6)
Not able to be seen or touched (10)
Of a son or daughter (6)
Overcome by force; conquered (7)
Peacemaker (8)
Preference based on prejudice (4)
Public; not hidden (5)
Real; genuine (9)
Rules proclaimed by one in authority (6)
Rushing headlong with a swaying motion (9)
Second generation; Japanese born in US before WWII (5)
Someone who takes the law into his own hands (9)
Squat; sit back on one's heels (6)
State of agitation or disturbance (7)
Surrender on certain conditions (10)
Tapering, four-sided structure with a pyramid-shaped top (7)
Third generation; Japanese born in US after WWII (6)
Very small rooms (8)
Violent (9)
Watching (5)

Farewell to Manzanar Vocabulary Word Search 2

```
C R E D O V E N T U R E T A D E S D T D
R D S B R B O M Z J G C H A K Z I W I T
W E M G A I L H R D L N G L N S M I N S
D A S T T R Z I E P S A U I P N P N G G
Y L R I U X R V H M T O E C V H D E J
V P L D G R D A J I V S R N O U B L L W
R O T E I N M V C C O S T S N C X E F T
V R X C S N E O Q K I N R K F O Q F V B
I V L N R A G D I N S W E J I N N I M Q
I M P A C T F V G L N R S G S G O L A G
C E P N I Z C F C O B K C C C E I I R Z
Z T D E S D L P I A V W I I A S T A O X
S N Q T R L E T A R R B N E T T A L O M
N A R S L I A A M T M E D S O I R E N Y
P L N U O D O Q L D R E E I R O G U E D
B I A S I V M U L I V I D N S N I S D M
J G S L E S E I S X S B A O I S M S I G
Z I A T A I G R J L N T A R Q N E I C F
Y V J P T I G J T C Y H C T C R G I T F
B X S G V Q R O T A C L P N H K N S K
```

A slight coloring (5)
Accepting what comes without complaint (8)
An over-crowded condition (10)
Authorities who take and keep things (12)
Beliefs (5)
Bring up (6)
Calm; serious (6)
Canceled (9)
Condition of being entirely forgotten (8)
Confirmation; support by facts (10)
Crouch in fear (6)
Dare to go (7)
Decision or choice (8)
Declared to be true (8)
Extremely angry (5)
First generation; born in Japan (5)
Forceful effect (6)
Going away in different directions (10)
Great confusion & disorder (5)
In an arrogant, domineering way (11)
Involuntary muscle contraction (5)
Keeping away (7)
Large, plain buildings used for temporary housing (8)
Left in a helpless condition (8)
Make or become smaller or fewer (7)

Male head of family (9)
Manner of standing (6)
Matter or point of discussion (5)
Narrow, open container holding water (6)
Non-citizens living in a country (6)
Nourishment or support (10)
Of a son or daughter (6)
One who wants things to be perfect (8)
Peacemaker (8)
Preference based on prejudice (4)
Public; not hidden (5)
Resettling in another country (10)
Rules proclaimed by one in authority (6)
Rushing headlong with a swaying motion (9)
Second generation; Japanese born in US before WWII (5)
Someone who takes the law into his own hands (9)
Squat; sit back on one's heels (6)
State of agitation or disturbance (7)
Third generation; Japanese born in US after WWII (6)
Watching (5)

Farewell to Manzanar Vocabulary Word Search 2 Answer Key

A slight coloring (5)
Accepting what comes without complaint (8)
An over-crowded condition (10)
Authorities who take and keep things (12)
Beliefs (5)
Bring up (6)
Calm; serious (6)
Canceled (9)
Condition of being entirely forgotten (8)
Confirmation; support by facts (10)
Crouch in fear (6)
Dare to go (7)
Decision or choice (8)
Declared to be true (8)
Extremely angry (5)
First generation; born in Japan (5)
Forceful effect (6)
Going away in different directions (10)
Great confusion & disorder (5)
In an arrogant, domineering way (11)
Involuntary muscle contraction (5)
Keeping away (7)
Large, plain buildings used for temporary housing (8)
Left in a helpless condition (8)
Make or become smaller or fewer (7)
Male head of family (9)
Manner of standing (6)
Matter or point of discussion (5)
Narrow, open container holding water (6)
Non-citizens living in a country (6)
Nourishment or support (10)
Of a son or daughter (6)
One who wants things to be perfect (8)
Peacemaker (8)
Preference based on prejudice (4)
Public; not hidden (5)
Resettling in another country (10)
Rules proclaimed by one in authority (6)
Rushing headlong with a swaying motion (9)
Second generation; Japanese born in US before WWII (5)
Someone who takes the law into his own hands (9)
Squat; sit back on one's heels (6)
State of agitation or disturbance (7)
Third generation; Japanese born in US after WWII (6)
Watching (5)

Farewell to Manzanar Vocabulary Word Search 3

```
G R O T E S Q U E M B B H G V P S P V P
R E R R D J I M M P L T U E H S S N U E
K S D E P R W M L A S U N D E R D X L T
Q E P F S V E M A P Y Z T K L L E G D N V
L R I P G I C A D T A U G E C N E N S E V
I V X N R A G Z Z G R C L R O M I E A R F
V O L I T I O N E E I T O I W G A N A W
I I C O U A O T E U Q R G D N O U S B R
D R R B R V N R G D A R H I E U T E I Q
O H E I B Z A G I M A F R N C G H I L X
B L D N U M S L I T L C S O N I E T I T
S M O E L N P J I B Y Q L I A N N U T D
T U Z V E R Q O Z D L L Q V T G T R Y W
I E S I N I N U X A E B I S S I M S C
N I U T G S B A B F T J L S P C O E T
A M B A E D Q S O L F S I B W A H I D Q
N P D B L N Z R U T I M U O K S A L A X
C E U L B I A S F E R F O I R N M O Z T X
E R E E V T E N J W M C I S P V S B E T
V I D P O T E N C Y E D Q U E S L I X M P
K O V R C V W Q S E D Q N G D E U G T T
C U B I C L E S U O N I M O H M I S I Q
P S T C I D E R S U O R G N O C N I R L
B L J Q S N O I T I N O M E R P G G R W
Z Y B E N E V O L E N T L O B E L I S K
```

AFFIRMED	GOUGING	OBLIVION	SURPLUS
ALIENS	GROTESQUE	OBSTINANCE	SUSTENANCE
ASUNDER	GUILELESS	OMINOUS	TINGE
AUTHENTIC	HUNKER	OVERT	TROUGH
BENEVOLENT	IMPACT	PLACATOR	TURBULENT
BIAS	IMPERIOUSLY	POTENCY	TURMOIL
CHAOS	INCONGRUOUS	PREMONITIONS	UNQUALIFIED
COLLABORATOR	INEVITABLE	PRIORITY	VALIDATION
CREDO	INTANGIBLE	RESERVOIR	VENTURE
CRINGE	ISSEI	RESIGNED	VIGIL
CUBICLES	ISSUE	SANSEI	VOLITION
DREDGE	LIVID	SEDATE	VULNERABILITY
DWINDLE	MAROONED	SPASM	
EDICTS	NISEI	STANCE	
EMIGRATION	OBELISK	SUBDUED	

Copyrighted

Farewell to Manzanar Vocabulary Word Search 3 Answer Key

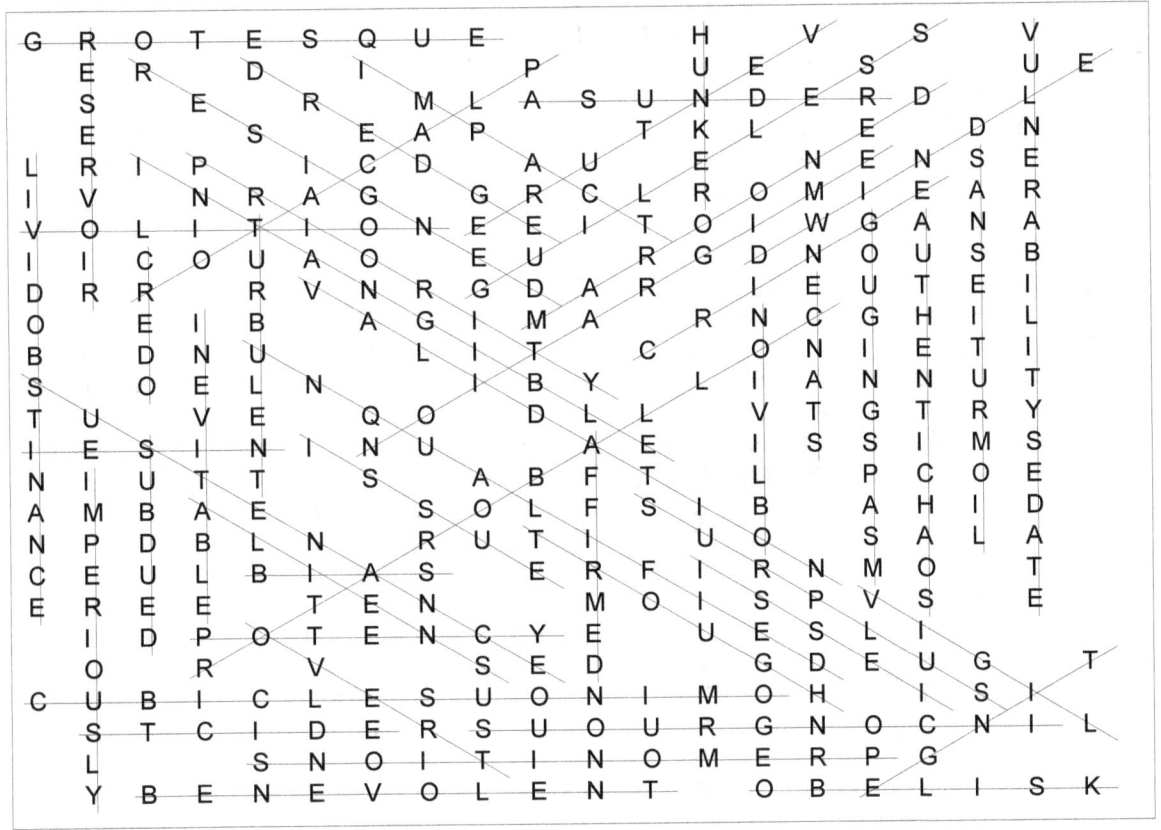

AFFIRMED	GOUGING	OBLIVION	SURPLUS
ALIENS	GROTESQUE	OBSTINANCE	SUSTENANCE
ASUNDER	GUILELESS	OMINOUS	TINGE
AUTHENTIC	HUNKER	OVERT	TROUGH
BENEVOLENT	IMPACT	PLACATOR	TURBULENT
BIAS	IMPERIOUSLY	POTENCY	TURMOIL
CHAOS	INCONGRUOUS	PREMONITIONS	UNQUALIFIED
COLLABORATOR	INEVITABLE	PRIORITY	VALIDATION
CREDO	INTANGIBLE	RESERVOIR	VENTURE
CRINGE	ISSEI	RESIGNED	VIGIL
CUBICLES	ISSUE	SANSEI	VOLITION
DREDGE	LIVID	SEDATE	VULNERABILITY
DWINDLE	MAROONED	SPASM	
EDICTS	NISEI	STANCE	
EMIGRATION	OBELISK	SUBDUED	

Farewell to Manzanar Vocabulary Word Search 4

```
A U T H E N T I C O N F I S C A T O R S
T U T P Y B T K R O T C A L P S O W H R L
H U N K E R I S S U T A Y T I R O I R M P
D C O Q Q Y N A D P X D N U O C A P M B
Z R I U L G N S Q E E X R M O H O O E L
Y I T E G A E T F M L S D B R N C S T A K
M N I S E I L C R O X I G U U G B T A X
Z G L N H L D I V O M R M L T E P H M Z
P E O A G I F E F P U P T E D S D U O V
V A V S B F N C A I F G O N N T E M R N
N E T V A E V C R L E M H T S I D O P V
O M N R B S T E O E I D G V E O N U H T
B I E X I X U N N D S F U L N I S O W
L G M V S A R R O T J O T L C S C Y S Z
I R N Q I I R U P S U E S N I T S Y I Z
V A R S G S C K L L R N E B A E S S N Y
I T E H E V I C H B U L E R U N R D N Y
O I T O P S A L I H X S I A C C G D R V
N O N B B R E G I T Z D L B S E F A E H
D N I I R E N R R V E N A I T U J T D Z
N X L A S A L E V U I D L L C S N E G H
S P B P T S V I D O G D V I I K P D E H
V P J N S O E B S T I S Z T D K S A E T
L K I L X F U I Q K R R P Y E R F R S R
G R O T E S Q U E C N A N E T S U S T M
```

AFFIRMED   EDICTS   NISEI   SPASM
ALIENS   EMIGRATION   OBELISK   STANCE
ASUNDER   FILIAL   OBLIVION   SUBDUED
AUTHENTIC   FLOURISH   OMINOUS   SURPLUS
BARRACKS   GROTESQUE   OVERT   SUSTENANCE
BENEVOLENT   HUNKER   PATRIARCH   TINGE
BIAS   IDEALIST   PLACATOR   TROUGH
CHAOS   IMPACT   POSTHUMOUS   TURBULENT
CONFISCATORS   INTANGIBLE   POTENCY   TURMOIL
CONGESTION   INTERNMENT   PRIORITY   UNQUALIFIED
CREDO   ISSEI   RESCINDED   VENTURE
CRINGE   ISSUE   RESERVOIR   VIGIL
CUBICLES   LIVID   SANSEI   VOLITION
DREDGE   METAMORPHOSIS   SEDATE   VULNERABILITY

Farewell to Manzanar Vocabulary Word Search 4 Answer Key

AFFIRMED	EDICTS	NISEI	SPASM
ALIENS	EMIGRATION	OBELISK	STANCE
ASUNDER	FILIAL	OBLIVION	SUBDUED
AUTHENTIC	FLOURISH	OMINOUS	SURPLUS
BARRACKS	GROTESQUE	OVERT	SUSTENANCE
BENEVOLENT	HUNKER	PATRIARCH	TINGE
BIAS	IDEALIST	PLACATOR	TROUGH
CHAOS	IMPACT	POSTHUMOUS	TURBULENT
CONFISCATORS	INTANGIBLE	POTENCY	TURMOIL
CONGESTION	INTERNMENT	PRIORITY	UNQUALIFIED
CREDO	ISSEI	RESCINDED	VENTURE
CRINGE	ISSUE	RESERVOIR	VIGIL
CUBICLES	LIVID	SANSEI	VOLITION
DREDGE	METAMORPHOSIS	SEDATE	VULNERABILITY

Farewell to Manzanar Vocabulary Crossword 1

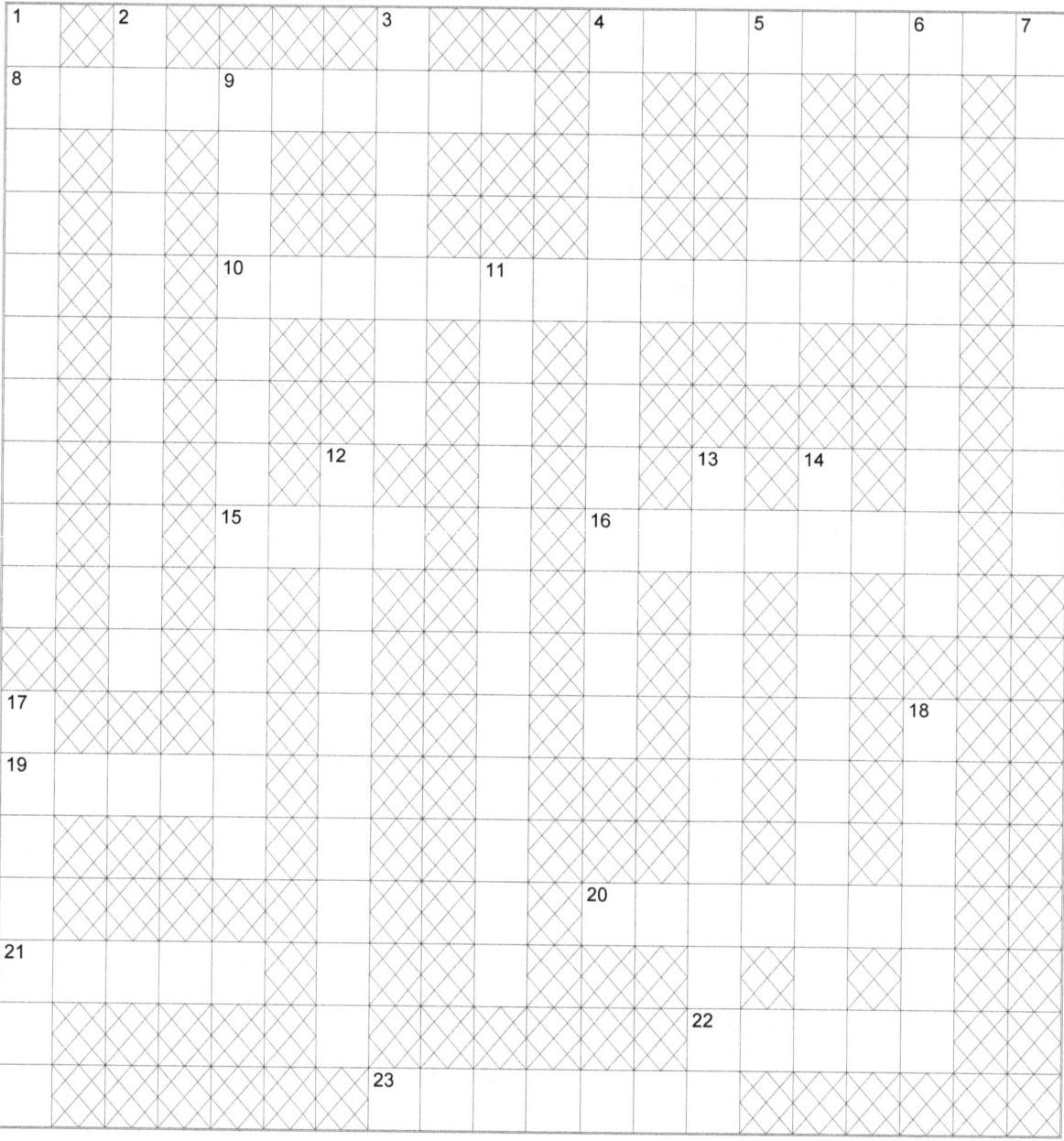

Across
4. Rushing headlong with a swaying motion
8. Kindly; charitable
10. Admitted to citizenship
15. Preference based on prejudice
16. State of agitation or disturbance
19. Public; not hidden
20. Unfavorable; threatening
21. First generation; born in Japan
22. Second generation; Japanese born in US before WWII
23. Extra

Down
1. Stubbornness
2. Out of place
3. Dare to go
4. Authorities who take and keep things
5. Rules proclaimed by one in authority
6. Not able to be seen or touched
7. Ridiculous; absurd
9. Being open to attack or injury
11. Agreement without objection
12. Confirmation; support by facts
13. Care taken beforehand
14. Happening after one's death
17. Digging; tearing out
18. Third generation; Japanese born in US after WWII

Farewell to Manzanar Vocabulary Crossword 1 Answer Key

	1 O		2 I			3 V		4 C	A	R	5 E	E	N	6 I	N	7 G
	8 B	E	N	E	V	O	L	E	N	T		O		D		N		R
	S		C			N		O			N		I		T		O
	T		O			T		N			F		C		A		T
	I		N	10 N	A	T	U	R	11 A	L	I	Z	A	T	I	O	N	E
	N		G	E			R		C		S		S			G		S
	A		R	R			E		Q		C				13		I		Q
	N		U	A		12 V		U		A		13 P		14 P		B		U
	C		O	15 B	I	A	S		I		16 T	U	R	M	O	I	L		E
	E		U	I		L			E		O		E		S		E	
			S	L		I			S		R		C		T			
17 G				I		D			C		S		A		H		18 S
19 O	V	E	R	T		A			E				U		U		A
U				Y		T			N				T		M		N
G						I			C		20 O	M	I	N	O	U	S
21 I	S	S	E	I		O			E		O			U		E
N						N					22 N	I	S	E	I
G					23 S	U	R	P	L	U	S

Across
- 4. Rushing headlong with a swaying motion
- 8. Kindly; charitable
- 10. Admitted to citizenship
- 15. Preference based on prejudice
- 16. State of agitation or disturbance
- 19. Public; not hidden
- 20. Unfavorable; threatening
- 21. First generation; born in Japan
- 22. Second generation; Japanese born in US before WWII
- 23. Extra

Down
- 1. Stubbornness
- 2. Out of place
- 3. Dare to go
- 4. Authorities who take and keep things
- 5. Rules proclaimed by one in authority
- 6. Not able to be seen or touched
- 7. Ridiculous; absurd
- 9. Being open to attack or injury
- 11. Agreement without objection
- 12. Confirmation; support by facts
- 13. Care taken beforehand
- 14. Happening after one's death
- 17. Digging; tearing out
- 18. Third generation; Japanese born in US after WWII

Farewell to Manzanar Vocabulary Crossword 2

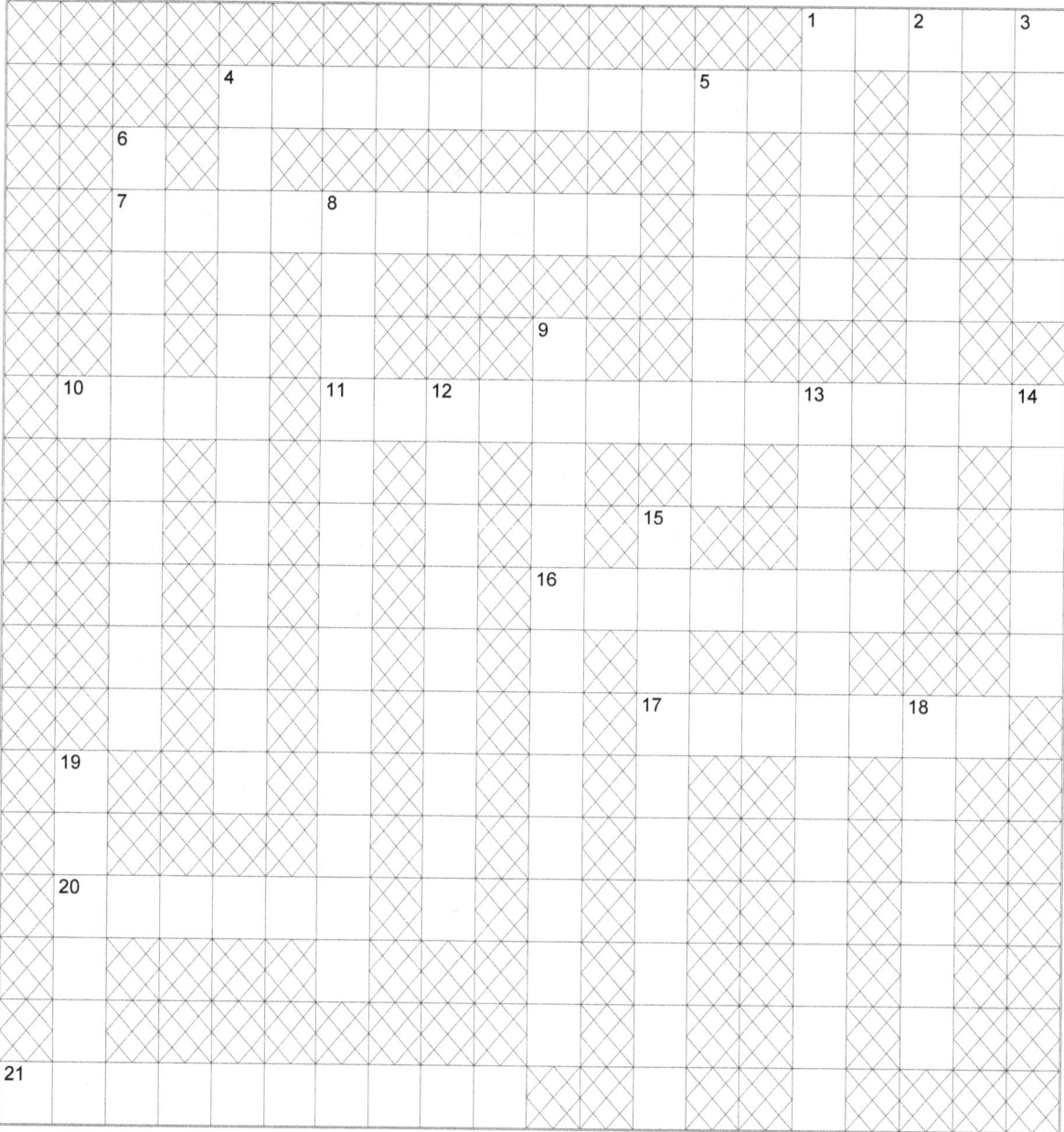

Across
1. Great confusion & disorder
4. Someone who works with the enemy, as with an enemy in one's country
7. Kindly; charitable
10. Preference based on prejudice
11. Admitted to citizenship
16. Unfavorable; threatening
17. Power; strength
20. Forceful effect
21. Become like the others in custom, etc.

Down
1. Beliefs
2. Stirring up public awareness and feeling
3. Involuntary muscle contraction
4. Authorities who take and keep things
5. State of agitation or disturbance
6. Stubbornness
8. Being open to attack or injury
9. Warnings of what is to come
12. Violent
13. Agreement without objection
14. Second generation; Japanese born in US before WWII
15. Going away in different directions
18. Crouch in fear
19. Non-citizens living in a country

Farewell to Manzanar Vocabulary Crossword 2 Answer Key

Across
1. Great confusion & disorder
4. Someone who works with the enemy, as with an enemy in one's country
7. Kindly; charitable
10. Preference based on prejudice
11. Admitted to citizenship
16. Unfavorable; threatening
17. Power; strength
20. Forceful effect
21. Become like the others in custom, etc.

Down
1. Beliefs
2. Stirring up public awareness and feeling
3. Involuntary muscle contraction
4. Authorities who take and keep things
5. State of agitation or disturbance
6. Stubbornness
8. Being open to attack or injury
9. Warnings of what is to come
12. Violent
13. Agreement without objection
14. Second generation; Japanese born in US before WWII
15. Going away in different directions
18. Crouch in fear
19. Non-citizens living in a country

Answers:

Across:
1. CHAOS
4. COLLABORATOR
7. BENEVOLENT
10. BIAS
11. NATURALIZATION
16. OMINOUS
17. POTENCY
20. IMPACT
21. ASSIMILATE

Down:
1. CONVICTIONS
2. AGITATING
3. SPASM
4. CONFISCATORS
5. TURMOIL
6. OBSTINACY
8. VULNERABILITY
9. PREMONITIONS
12. RIOTOUS
13. ACQUIESCENCE
14. NISEI
15. DISPERSING
18. CRINGE
19. ALIEN

Farewell To Manzanar Vocabulary Crossword 3

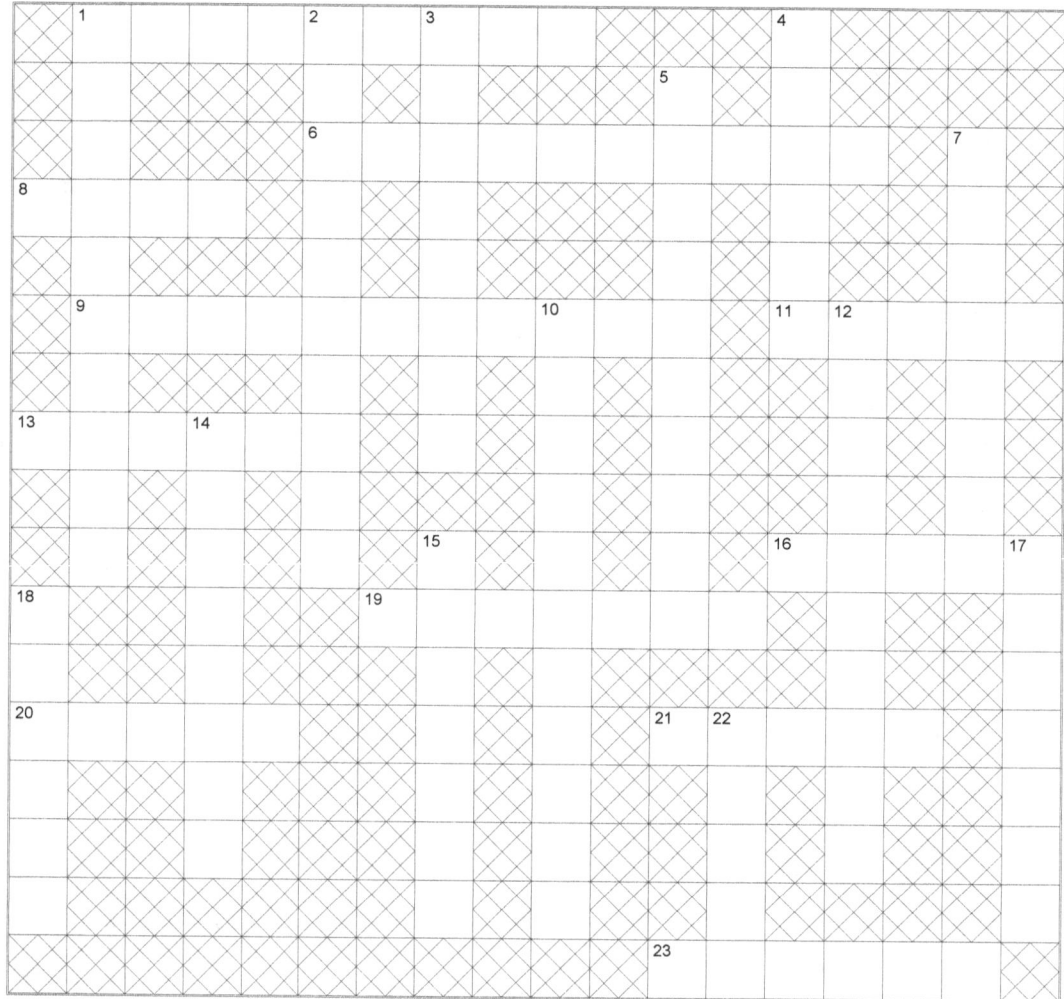

Across
1. Rushing headlong with a swaying motion
6. Unavoidable
8. Preference based on prejudice
9. Complete; without lines or restrictions
11. Extremely angry
13. Third generation; Japanese born in US after WWII
16. Beliefs
19. Digging; tearing out
20. First generation; born in Japan
21. Second generation; Japanese born in US before WWII
23. Calm, serious

Down
1. Surrender on certain conditions
2. Resettling in another country
3. One who wants things to be perfect
4. Of a son or daughter
5. Confirmation; support by facts
7. Declared to be true
10. Out of place
12. Being forced to stay in a place
14. Person who harms an enemy nation
15. Power; strength
17. Tapering, four-sided structure with a pyramid-shaped top
18. Rules proclaimed by one in authority
22. Matter or point of discussion

Farewell To Manzanar Vocabulary Crossword 3 Answer Key

	1 C	A	R	E	2 E	N	3 I	N	G		4 F			
	A				M		D			5 V	I			
	P			6 I	N	E	V	I	T	A	B	L	E	7 A
8 B	I	A	S		G		A			L		I		F
	T				R		L			I		A		F
	9 U	N	Q	U	A	L	I	10 F	I	E	D	11 L	12 I	V	I	D
	L				T		S		N			A		N		R
13 S	A	N	14 S	E	I		T		C			T		T		M
	T		A		O				C			I		E		E
	E		B		N		15 P		N			16 C	R	E	D	17 O
18 E			O			19 G	O	U	G	I	N	G		N		B
D			T				T		R					M		E
20 I	S	S	E	I			E		U		21 N	22 I	S	E	I	L
C			U				N		O			S		N		I
T			R				C		U			S		T		S
S							Y		S			U				K
										23 S	E	D	A	T	E	

Across
1. Rushing headlong with a swaying motion
6. Unavoidable
8. Preference based on prejudice
9. Complete; without lines or restrictions
11. Extremely angry
13. Third generation; Japanese born in US after WWII
16. Beliefs
19. Digging; tearing out
20. First generation; born in Japan
21. Second generation; Japanese born in US before WWII
23. Calm; serious

Down
1. Surrender on certain conditions
2. Resettling in another country
3. One who wants things to be perfect
4. Of a son or daughter
5. Confirmation; support by facts
7. Declared to be true
10. Out of place
12. Being forced to stay in a place
14. Person who harms an enemy nation
15. Power; strength
17. Tapering, four-sided structure with a pyramid-shaped top
18. Rules proclaimed by one in authority
22. Matter or point of discussion

Farewell to Manzanar Vocabulary Crossword 4

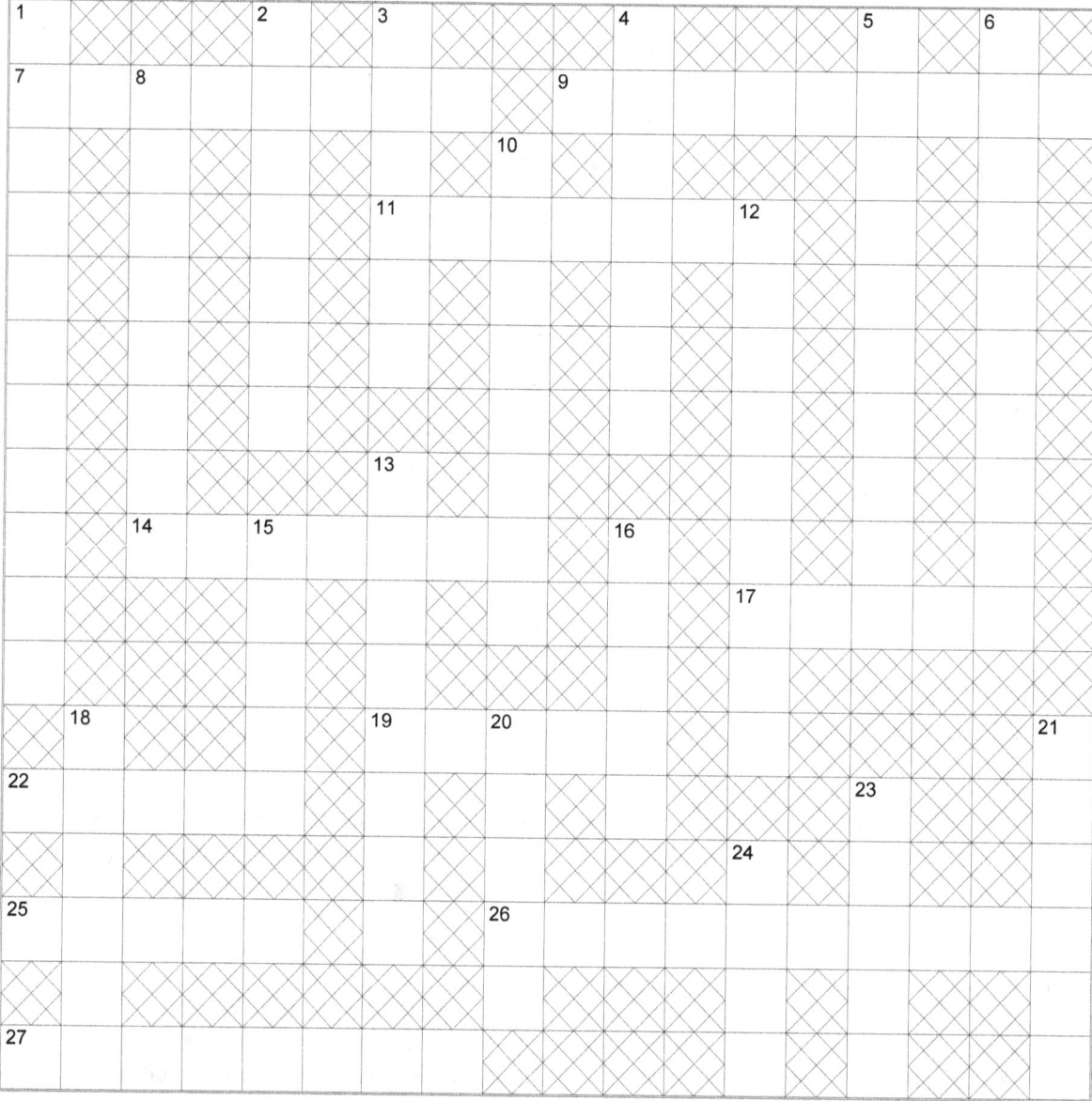

Across
7. Left in a helpless condition
9. Rushing headlong with a swaying motion
11. In pieces or separate parts
14. Make or become smaller or fewer
17. Public; not hidden
19. Extremely angry
22. Second generation; Japanese born in US before WWII
25. A slight coloring
26. Unavoidable
27. Peacemaker

Down
1. In an arrogant, domineering way
2. Power; strength
3. Calm; serious
4. Keeping away
5. Not able to be seen or touched
6. Being forced to stay in a place
8. Accepting what comes without complaint
10. Very small rooms
12. Place where water is collected and stored
13. One who wants things to be perfect
15. First generation; born in Japan
16. Beliefs
18. Of a son or daughter
20. Watching
21. Non-citizens living in a country
23. Great confusion & disorder
24. Preference based on prejudice

Farewell to Manzanar Vocabulary Crossword 4 Answer Key

	1 I			2 P		3 S			4 W			5 I		6 I	
7 M	A	8 R	O	O	N	E	D		9 C	A	R	E	E	N	I	N	G
	P		E		T		D		10 C		R			T		T	
	E		S		E		11 A	S	U	N	D	E	12 R		A		E
	R		I		N		T		B		I		E		N		R
	I		G		C		E		I		N		S		G		N
	O		N		Y		13 I		C		G		E		I		M
	U		E				I		L				R		B		E
	S		14 D	15 W	I	N	D	L	E		16 C		V		L		N
	L			I			E		S		R		17 O	V	E	R	T
	Y			S			A				E		I				
		18 F		S		19 L	I	20 V	I	D		R				21 A
22 N	I	S	E	I		I		I		O				23 C		L
		L				S		G				24 B		H		I
25 T	I	N	G	E		T		26 I	N	E	V	I	T	A	B	L	E
		A						L				A		O		N
27 P	L	A	C	A	T	O	R					S		S		S

Across
7. Left in a helpless condition
9. Rushing headlong with a swaying motion
11. In pieces or separate parts
14. Make or become smaller or fewer
17. Public; not hidden
19. Extremely angry
22. Second generation; Japanese born in US before WWII
25. A slight coloring
26. Unavoidable
27. Peacemaker

Down
1. In an arrogant, domineering way
2. Power; strength
3. Calm; serious
4. Keeping away
5. Not able to be seen or touched
6. Being forced to stay in a place
8. Accepting what comes without complaint
10. Very small rooms
12. Place where water is collected and stored
13. One who wants things to be perfect
15. First generation; born in Japan
16. Beliefs
18. Of a son or daughter
20. Watching
21. Non-citizens living in a country
23. Great confusion & disorder
24. Preference based on prejudice

Farewell to Manzanar Vocabulary Juggle Letters 1

1. ETNIAIBLNG = 1. _____
   Not able to be seen or touched

2. OTUILNTARAANZI = 2. _____
   Admitted to citizenship

3. TMIAESIALS = 3. _____
   Become like the others in custom, etc.

4. SSEIU = 4. _____
   Matter or point of discussion

5. NUESCSTANE = 5. _____
   Nourishment or support

6. GINAWRD = 6. _____
   Keeping away

7. ENCTAS = 7. _____
   Manner of standing

8. KSACRARB = 8. _____
   Large, plain buildings used for temporary housing

9. PMSSA = 9. _____
   Involuntary muscle contraction

10. SNPIOIETNOMR =10. _____
    Warnings of what is to come

11. VNOOILBI =11. _____
    Condition of being entirely forgotten

12. MPTCAI =12. _____
    Forceful effect

13. TCAUALIPET =13. _____
    Surrender on certain conditions

14. MSRELIIUOYP =14. _____
    In an arrogant, domineering way

15. IGENT =15. _____
    A slight coloring

Farewell to Manzanar Vocabulary Juggle Letters 1 Answer Key

1. ETNIAIBLNG = 1. INTANGIBLE
   Not able to be seen or touched

2. OTUILNTARAANZI = 2. NATURALIZATION
   Admitted to citizenship

3. TMIAESIALS = 3. ASSIMILATE
   Become like the others in custom, etc.

4. SSEIU = 4. ISSUE
   Matter or point of discussion

5. NUESCSTANE = 5. SUSTENANCE
   Nourishment or support

6. GINAWRD = 6. WARDING
   Keeping away

7. ENCTAS = 7. STANCE
   Manner of standing

8. KSACRARB = 8. BARRACKS
   Large, plain buildings used for temporary housing

9. PMSSA = 9. SPASM
   Involuntary muscle contraction

10. SNPIOIETNOMR = 10. PREMONITIONS
    Warnings of what is to come

11. VNOOILBI = 11. OBLIVION
    Condition of being entirely forgotten

12. MPTCAI = 12. IMPACT
    Forceful effect

13. TCAUALIPET = 13. CAPITULATE
    Surrender on certain conditions

14. MSRELIIUOYP = 14. IMPERIOUSLY
    In an arrogant, domineering way

15. IGENT = 15. TINGE
    A slight coloring

Farewell to Manzanar Vocabulary Juggle Letters 2

1. IBOTNCSNAE = 1. _____
   Stubbornness

2. RIOTULM = 2. _____
   State of agitation or disturbance

3. RAEIFDMF = 3. _____
   Declared to be true

4. TDLIISEA = 4. _____
   One who wants things to be perfect

5. LSPURUS = 5. _____
   Extra

6. CRTPALAO = 6. _____
   Peacemaker

7. EDISGNRE = 7. _____
   Accepting what comes without complaint

8. SKLIEBO = 8. _____
   Tapering, four-sided structure with a pyramid-shaped top

9. AIIFLL = 9. _____
   Of a son or daughter

10. SUIECLCB =10. _____
    Very small rooms

11. OONIMSU =11. _____
    Unfavorable; threatening

12. ROMINIESPOTN =12. _____
    Warnings of what is to come

13. RPITROYI =13. _____
    Coming in order of importance

14. ECNRGI =14. _____
    Crouch in fear

15. SIECDT =15. _____
    Rules proclaimed by one in authority

Copyrighted

Farewell to Manzanar Vocabulary Juggle Letters 2 Answer Key

1. IBOTNCSNAE = 1. OBSTINANCE
   Stubbornness

2. RIOTULM = 2. TURMOIL
   State of agitation or disturbance

3. RAEIFDMF = 3. AFFIRMED
   Declared to be true

4. TDLIISEA = 4. IDEALIST
   One who wants things to be perfect

5. LSPURUS = 5. SURPLUS
   Extra

6. CRTPALAO = 6. PLACATOR
   Peacemaker

7. EDISGNRE = 7. RESIGNED
   Accepting what comes without complaint

8. SKLIEBO = 8. OBELISK
   Tapering, four-sided structure with a pyramid-shaped top

9. AIIFLL = 9. FILIAL
   Of a son or daughter

10. SUIECLCB = 10. CUBICLES
    Very small rooms

11. OONIMSU = 11. OMINOUS
    Unfavorable; threatening

12. ROMINIESPOTN = 12. PREMONITIONS
    Warnings of what is to come

13. RPITROYI = 13. PRIORITY
    Coming in order of importance

14. ECNRGI = 14. CRINGE
    Crouch in fear

15. SIECDT = 15. EDICTS
    Rules proclaimed by one in authority

Farewell to Manzanar Vocabulary Juggle Letters 3

1. TDLAESII = 1. _____
   One who wants things to be perfect

2. URTOBEAS = 2. _____
   Person who harms an enemy nation

3. ATRNTZAUIOALIN = 3. _____
   Admitted to citizenship

4. NARGTEOIMI = 4. _____
   Resettling in another country

5. GSNOTIENOC = 5. _____
   An over-crowded condition

6. TROEV = 6. _____
   Public; not hidden

7. NEUTERV = 7. _____
   Dare to go

8. SBLEOIK = 8. _____
   Tapering, four-sided structure with a pyramid-shaped top

9. TOLACRPA = 9. _____
   Peacemaker

10. EVNENELOBT =10. _____
    Kindly; charitable

11. AICRPONSETU =11. _____
    Care taken beforehand

12. ESLUGILSE =12. _____
    Honest; straightforward

13. SSIIE =13. _____
    First generation; born in Japan

14. LISEAN =14. _____
    Non-citizens living in a country

15. TTUHIANCE =15. _____
    Real; genuine

Farewell to Manzanar Vocabulary Juggle Letters 3 Answer Key

1. TDLAESII = 1. IDEALIST
One who wants things to be perfect

2. URTOBEAS = 2. SABOTEUR
Person who harms an enemy nation

3. ATRNTZAUIOALIN = 3. NATURALIZATION
Admitted to citizenship

4. NARGTEOIMI = 4. EMIGRATION
Resettling in another country

5. GSNOTIENOC = 5. CONGESTION
An over-crowded condition

6. TROEV = 6. OVERT
Public; not hidden

7. NEUTERV = 7. VENTURE
Dare to go

8. SBLEOIK = 8. OBELISK
Tapering, four-sided structure with a pyramid-shaped top

9. TOLACRPA = 9. PLACATOR
Peacemaker

10. EVNENELOBT = 10. BENEVOLENT
Kindly; charitable

11. AICRPONSETU = 11. PRECAUTIONS
Care taken beforehand

12. ESLUGILSE = 12. GUILELESS
Honest; straightforward

13. SSIIE = 13. ISSEI
First generation; born in Japan

14. LISEAN = 14. ALIENS
Non-citizens living in a country

15. TTUHIANCE = 15. AUTHENTIC
Real; genuine

Farewell to Manzanar Vocabulary Juggle Letters 4

1. RBASKRAC = 1. _____
   Large, plain buildings used for temporary housing

2. RAOEBSTU = 2. _____
   Person who harms an enemy nation

3. IEOTUSPRACN = 3. _____
   Care taken beforehand

4. UOIRSHFL = 4. _____
   A showy display

5. RHCPIRATA = 5. _____
   Male head of family

6. IGILV = 6. _____
   Watching

7. NRUDSEA = 7. _____
   In pieces or separate parts

8. SEISU = 8. _____
   Matter or point of discussion

9. NREEICAGN = 9. _____
   Rushing headlong with a swaying motion

10. AALLCOTOORBR = 10. _____
    Someone who works with the enemy, as with an enemy in one's country

11. BDDSUUE = 11. _____
    Overcome by force; conquered

12. GIATNTIGA = 12. _____
    Stirring up public awareness and feeling

13. TERVO = 13. _____
    Public; not hidden

14. OOPESASMRTMHI = 14. _____
    Change of form or structure

15. SVRIRREEO = 15. _____
    Place where water is collected and stored

Farewell to Manzanar Vocabulary Juggle Letters 4 Answer Key

1. RBASKRAC = 1. BARRACKS
   Large, plain buildings used for temporary housing

2. RAOEBSTU = 2. SABOTEUR
   Person who harms an enemy nation

3. IEOTUSPRACN = 3. PRECAUTIONS
   Care taken beforehand

4. UOIRSHFL = 4. FLOURISH
   A showy display

5. RHCPIRATA = 5. PATRIARCH
   Male head of family

6. IGILV = 6. VIGIL
   Watching

7. NRUDSEA = 7. ASUNDER
   In pieces or separate parts

8. SEISU = 8. ISSUE
   Matter or point of discussion

9. NREEICAGN = 9. CAREENING
   Rushing headlong with a swaying motion

10. AALLCOTOORBR = 10. COLLABORATOR
    Someone who works with the enemy, as with an enemy in one's country

11. BDDSUUE = 11. SUBDUED
    Overcome by force; conquered

12. GIATNTIGA = 12. AGITATING
    Stirring up public awareness and feeling

13. TERVO = 13. OVERT
    Public; not hidden

14. OOPESASMRTMHI = 14. METAMORPHOSIS
    Change of form or structure

15. SVRIRREEO = 15. RESERVOIR
    Place where water is collected and stored

ACQUIESCENCE	Agreement without objection
AFFIRMED	Declared to be true
AGITATING	Stirring up public awareness and feeling
ALIENS	Non-citizens living in a country
ASSIMILATE	Become like the others in custom, etc.
ASUNDER	In pieces or separate parts

AUTHENTIC	Real; genuine
BARRACKS	Large, plain buildings used for temporary housing
BENEVOLENT	Kindly; charitable
BIAS	Preference based on prejudice
CAPITULATE	Surrender on certain conditions
CAREENING	Rushing headlong with a swaying motion

CHAOS	Great confusion & disorder
COLLABORATOR	Someone who works with the enemy, as with an enemy in one's country
CONFISCATORS	Authorities who take and keep things
CONGESTION	An over-crowded condition
CREDO	Beliefs
CRINGE	Crouch in fear

CUBICLES	Very small rooms
DISPERSING	Going away in different directions
DREDGE	Bring up
DWINDLE	Make or become smaller or fewer
EDICTS	Rules proclaimed by one in authority
EMIGRATION	Resettling in another country

FILIAL	Of a son or daughter
FLOURISH	A showy display
GOUGING	Digging; tearing out
GROTESQUE	Ridiculous; absurd
GUILELESS	Honest; straightforward
HUNKER	Squat; sit back on one's heels

IDEALIST	One who wants things to be perfect
IMPACT	Forceful effect
IMPERIOUSLY	In an arrogant, domineering way
INCONGRUOUS	Out of place
INEVITABLE	Unavoidable
INTANGIBLE	Not able to be seen or touched

INTERNMENT	Being forced to stay in a place
ISSEI	First generation; born in Japan
ISSUE	Matter or point of discussion
LIVID	Extremely angry
MAROONED	Left in a helpless condition
METAMORPHOSIS	Change of form or structure

NATURALIZATION	Admitted to citizenship
NISEI	Second generation; Japanese born in US before WWII
OBELISK	Tapering, four-sided structure with a pyramid-shaped top
OBLIVION	Condition of being entirely forgotten
OBSTINANCE	Stubbornness
OMINOUS	Unfavorable; threatening

OVERT	Public; not hidden
PATRIARCH	Male head of family
PLACATOR	Peacemaker
POSTHUMOUS	Happening after one's death
POTENCY	Power; strength
PRECAUTIONS	Care taken beforehand

PREMONITIONS	Warnings of what is to come
PRIORITY	Coming in order of importance
RESCINDED	Canceled
RESERVOIR	Place where water is collected and stored
RESIGNED	Accepting what comes without complaint
SABOTEUR	Person who harms an enemy nation

SANSEI	Third generation; Japanese born in US after WWII
SEDATE	Calm; serious
SPASM	Involuntary muscle contraction
STANCE	Manner of standing
SUBDUED	Overcome by force; conquered
SURPLUS	Extra

SUSTENANCE	Nourishment or support
TINGE	A slight coloring
TROUGH	Narrow, open container holding water
TURBULENT	Violent
TURMOIL	State of agitation or disturbance
UNQUALIFIED	Complete; without lines or restrictions

VALIDATION	Confirmation; support by facts
VENTURE	Dare to go
VIGIL	Watching
VIGILANTE	Someone who takes the law into his own hands
VOLITION	Decision or choice
VULNERABILITY	Being open to attack or injury

WARDING

Keeping away

Farewell to Manzanar Vocabulary

SURPLUS	PATRIARCH	AFFIRMED	EDICTS	POTENCY
METAMORPHOSIS	INEVITABLE	EMIGRATION	ALIENS	PRECAUTIONS
MAROONED	INTANGIBLE	FREE SPACE	IMPERIOUSLY	SEDATE
OMINOUS	PREMONITIONS	IMPACT	CUBICLES	SPASM
DWINDLE	SUBDUED	VALIDATION	SUSTENANCE	CREDO

Farewell to Manzanar Vocabulary

DISPERSING	BENEVOLENT	SABOTEUR	INTERNMENT	CONFISCATORS
ACQUIESCENCE	STANCE	FILIAL	TINGE	GUILELESS
OBSTINANCE	LIVID	FREE SPACE	CAREENING	TROUGH
BARRACKS	IDEALIST	POSTHUMOUS	AUTHENTIC	OVERT
RESERVOIR	AGITATING	FLOURISH	VIGIL	RESIGNED

Farewell to Manzanar Vocabulary

VIGIL	SUBDUED	ASUNDER	ACQUIESCENCE	VIGILANTE
RESERVOIR	OBLIVION	EMIGRATION	IDEALIST	PRIORITY
CAREENING	VALIDATION	FREE SPACE	BENEVOLENT	OMINOUS
SUSTENANCE	RESIGNED	CAPITULATE	UNQUALIFIED	CUBICLES
LIVID	ALIENS	GROTESQUE	DISPERSING	GOUGING

Farewell to Manzanar Vocabulary

IMPERIOUSLY	SABOTEUR	POSTHUMOUS	POTENCY	PRECAUTIONS
OBELISK	TROUGH	CRINGE	EDICTS	IMPACT
PREMONITIONS	MAROONED	FREE SPACE	TINGE	OBSTINANCE
INTANGIBLE	INEVITABLE	SURPLUS	SPASM	RESCINDED
NISEI	SEDATE	GUILELESS	DWINDLE	AFFIRMED

Farewell to Manzanar Vocabulary

VULNERABILITY	SANSEI	BENEVOLENT	VENTURE	NATURALIZATION
EMIGRATION	WARDING	SUBDUED	EDICTS	OBELISK
ACQUIESCENCE	CONGESTION	FREE SPACE	DISPERSING	ASSIMILATE
INTERNMENT	IDEALIST	SABOTEUR	VALIDATION	POTENCY
RESERVOIR	DREDGE	FLOURISH	DWINDLE	CREDO

Farewell to Manzanar Vocabulary

COLLABORATOR	MAROONED	CRINGE	GROTESQUE	INEVITABLE
ASUNDER	BARRACKS	VIGIL	IMPACT	AUTHENTIC
TURMOIL	OBLIVION	FREE SPACE	SURPLUS	TURBULENT
AGITATING	CAPITULATE	PRECAUTIONS	HUNKER	VOLITION
PRIORITY	BIAS	CUBICLES	METAMORPHOSIS	UNQUALIFIED

Farewell to Manzanar Vocabulary

SUBDUED	VULNERABILITY	DREDGE	TROUGH	SURPLUS
ALIENS	DWINDLE	SABOTEUR	PREMONITIONS	INTANGIBLE
SEDATE	INCONGRUOUS	FREE SPACE	VOLITION	TURMOIL
OVERT	ASSIMILATE	OMINOUS	BENEVOLENT	VIGILANTE
PRIORITY	PRECAUTIONS	BIAS	NISEI	HUNKER

Farewell to Manzanar Vocabulary

UNQUALIFIED	DISPERSING	ACQUIESCENCE	GROTESQUE	EMIGRATION
IDEALIST	CONFISCATORS	RESERVOIR	CREDO	METAMORPHOSIS
TURBULENT	OBSTINANCE	FREE SPACE	SPASM	CRINGE
FILIAL	VENTURE	VIGIL	BARRACKS	IMPACT
CHAOS	AGITATING	PATRIARCH	ISSUE	NATURALIZATION

Farewell to Manzanar Vocabulary

EDICTS	ASUNDER	FLOURISH	SUBDUED	OMINOUS
METAMORPHOSIS	STANCE	LIVID	INTANGIBLE	RESCINDED
INEVITABLE	VALIDATION	FREE SPACE	SUSTENANCE	VULNERABILITY
DWINDLE	VOLITION	TURMOIL	ISSUE	TINGE
RESERVOIR	GROTESQUE	CONFISCATORS	INTERNMENT	NISEI

Farewell to Manzanar Vocabulary

SANSEI	ASSIMILATE	NATURALIZATION	ACQUIESCENCE	COLLABORATOR
CAPITULATE	ISSEI	RESIGNED	EMIGRATION	MAROONED
TROUGH	SPASM	FREE SPACE	SABOTEUR	OBLIVION
OBSTINANCE	PREMONITIONS	FILIAL	ALIENS	INCONGRUOUS
AGITATING	IDEALIST	CHAOS	CUBICLES	BIAS

Farewell to Manzanar Vocabulary

TURMOIL	CONGESTION	POTENCY	VENTURE	BIAS
GOUGING	SUBDUED	TURBULENT	MAROONED	PREMONITIONS
ACQUIESCENCE	INTANGIBLE	FREE SPACE	OMINOUS	EDICTS
AUTHENTIC	PRIORITY	INTERNMENT	FILIAL	BARRACKS
ISSEI	HUNKER	PLACATOR	TINGE	DISPERSING

Farewell to Manzanar Vocabulary

UNQUALIFIED	CUBICLES	PRECAUTIONS	VOLITION	IMPERIOUSLY
CAREENING	CRINGE	VULNERABILITY	PATRIARCH	SUSTENANCE
POSTHUMOUS	ASUNDER	FREE SPACE	METAMORPHOSIS	CHAOS
WARDING	VALIDATION	DWINDLE	OBLIVION	IDEALIST
LIVID	NATURALIZATION	CONFISCATORS	OVERT	RESCINDED

Farewell to Manzanar Vocabulary

EDICTS	CREDO	DWINDLE	FILIAL	GUILELESS
EMIGRATION	SANSEI	ASSIMILATE	NATURALIZATION	WARDING
DISPERSING	IMPACT	FREE SPACE	ASUNDER	PRIORITY
CRINGE	VENTURE	INTERNMENT	GOUGING	UNQUALIFIED
RESIGNED	SABOTEUR	COLLABORATOR	TINGE	VOLITION

Farewell to Manzanar Vocabulary

OBLIVION	HUNKER	CONGESTION	ALIENS	BARRACKS
OBELISK	FLOURISH	OVERT	NISEI	CHAOS
CONFISCATORS	GROTESQUE	FREE SPACE	SUSTENANCE	IDEALIST
AGITATING	POTENCY	VIGILANTE	INTANGIBLE	INCONGRUOUS
MAROONED	PREMONITIONS	SEDATE	BENEVOLENT	ACQUIESCENCE

Farewell to Manzanar Vocabulary

COLLABORATOR	TURBULENT	RESCINDED	IMPACT	TINGE
DISPERSING	GROTESQUE	METAMORPHOSIS	TURMOIL	IMPERIOUSLY
CAPITULATE	SANSEI	FREE SPACE	RESERVOIR	CUBICLES
SURPLUS	AGITATING	OBELISK	UNQUALIFIED	OBSTINANCE
ACQUIESCENCE	NISEI	INEVITABLE	ISSUE	POTENCY

Farewell to Manzanar Vocabulary

VIGILANTE	VENTURE	CONGESTION	BARRACKS	GUILELESS
CHAOS	AUTHENTIC	SEDATE	INTANGIBLE	BIAS
VIGIL	VALIDATION	FREE SPACE	WARDING	SUBDUED
STANCE	DWINDLE	SUSTENANCE	CAREENING	DREDGE
VOLITION	ASUNDER	ISSEI	ASSIMILATE	EDICTS

Farewell to Manzanar Vocabulary

ACQUIESCENCE	ASSIMILATE	INTERNMENT	GROTESQUE	BENEVOLENT
PRIORITY	PRECAUTIONS	OBSTINANCE	POSTHUMOUS	EMIGRATION
TURMOIL	SUSTENANCE	FREE SPACE	BIAS	UNQUALIFIED
PREMONITIONS	STANCE	ISSUE	MAROONED	IMPERIOUSLY
AUTHENTIC	RESCINDED	OMINOUS	SANSEI	TURBULENT

Farewell to Manzanar Vocabulary

NATURALIZATION	TROUGH	GOUGING	PATRIARCH	VOLITION
OVERT	CHAOS	VALIDATION	LIVID	CAPITULATE
VULNERABILITY	RESERVOIR	FREE SPACE	SPASM	VIGIL
COLLABORATOR	POTENCY	BARRACKS	SUBDUED	WARDING
CUBICLES	DISPERSING	AFFIRMED	SURPLUS	CAREENING

Farewell to Manzanar Vocabulary

DWINDLE	SPASM	SUSTENANCE	ALIENS	FILIAL
INTANGIBLE	PATRIARCH	CAPITULATE	NISEI	OBSTINANCE
VENTURE	CAREENING	FREE SPACE	IMPACT	AFFIRMED
WARDING	SANSEI	ASUNDER	GUILELESS	VALIDATION
CRINGE	GROTESQUE	TURMOIL	POSTHUMOUS	CONGESTION

Farewell to Manzanar Vocabulary

BARRACKS	PRECAUTIONS	PLACATOR	TINGE	SUBDUED
VIGIL	SURPLUS	SEDATE	VOLITION	INCONGRUOUS
HUNKER	OBELISK	FREE SPACE	STANCE	CUBICLES
PREMONITIONS	CONFISCATORS	OMINOUS	IDEALIST	TROUGH
AGITATING	RESIGNED	NATURALIZATION	TURBULENT	COLLABORATOR

Farewell to Manzanar Vocabulary

BARRACKS	IMPACT	WARDING	SUSTENANCE	CHAOS
OBSTINANCE	ISSEI	RESERVOIR	INTANGIBLE	MAROONED
SANSEI	BIAS	FREE SPACE	ASUNDER	DISPERSING
VIGIL	PRECAUTIONS	SURPLUS	PREMONITIONS	EDICTS
VULNERABILITY	TURBULENT	GUILELESS	VENTURE	IMPERIOUSLY

Farewell to Manzanar Vocabulary

TINGE	HUNKER	ACQUIESCENCE	RESIGNED	ISSUE
GOUGING	ASSIMILATE	AFFIRMED	CREDO	EMIGRATION
POTENCY	VIGILANTE	FREE SPACE	CUBICLES	VALIDATION
NATURALIZATION	PLACATOR	PATRIARCH	VOLITION	CAPITULATE
IDEALIST	TROUGH	AGITATING	TURMOIL	FLOURISH

Farewell to Manzanar Vocabulary

CAPITULATE	VALIDATION	STANCE	RESERVOIR	POSTHUMOUS
PRECAUTIONS	GROTESQUE	VIGIL	BIAS	CRINGE
TROUGH	AGITATING	FREE SPACE	DREDGE	CREDO
PLACATOR	TINGE	ISSUE	CUBICLES	IDEALIST
VENTURE	BENEVOLENT	CHAOS	CAREENING	FLOURISH

Farewell to Manzanar Vocabulary

VULNERABILITY	PREMONITIONS	INEVITABLE	ASUNDER	VOLITION
PATRIARCH	SUSTENANCE	IMPACT	ACQUIESCENCE	HUNKER
SEDATE	UNQUALIFIED	FREE SPACE	OBLIVION	GUILELESS
BARRACKS	AUTHENTIC	GOUGING	OBSTINANCE	NISEI
DISPERSING	VIGILANTE	TURMOIL	OVERT	CONGESTION

Farewell to Manzanar Vocabulary

CONFISCATORS	AFFIRMED	SEDATE	VENTURE	AUTHENTIC
GROTESQUE	OMINOUS	COLLABORATOR	CUBICLES	GUILELESS
SANSEI	ISSUE	FREE SPACE	RESIGNED	IMPACT
TURBULENT	VULNERABILITY	SURPLUS	SUSTENANCE	EDICTS
RESCINDED	NATURALIZATION	SABOTEUR	PRECAUTIONS	SUBDUED

Farewell to Manzanar Vocabulary

DISPERSING	TROUGH	LIVID	PATRIARCH	ASSIMILATE
CRINGE	SPASM	VIGIL	WARDING	POTENCY
VIGILANTE	IMPERIOUSLY	FREE SPACE	VOLITION	CREDO
FILIAL	INTERNMENT	INTANGIBLE	ALIENS	CAREENING
GOUGING	UNQUALIFIED	AGITATING	OBELISK	IDEALIST

Farewell to Manzanar Vocabulary

PRECAUTIONS	METAMORPHOSIS	OBELISK	POSTHUMOUS	CONGESTION
VIGILANTE	BENEVOLENT	DISPERSING	UNQUALIFIED	SURPLUS
VENTURE	POTENCY	FREE SPACE	OBSTINANCE	PRIORITY
SANSEI	PLACATOR	CREDO	GROTESQUE	OMINOUS
ISSEI	INCONGRUOUS	OBLIVION	GUILELESS	PREMONITIONS

Farewell to Manzanar Vocabulary

TURMOIL	NISEI	AUTHENTIC	NATURALIZATION	AGITATING
CONFISCATORS	IMPERIOUSLY	IMPACT	VALIDATION	ALIENS
ISSUE	CRINGE	FREE SPACE	TINGE	VULNERABILITY
HUNKER	AFFIRMED	PATRIARCH	ASSIMILATE	BARRACKS
CHAOS	SABOTEUR	VIGIL	SEDATE	ASUNDER

Farewell to Manzanar Vocabulary

UNQUALIFIED	AFFIRMED	OBELISK	WARDING	IMPERIOUSLY
SURPLUS	GROTESQUE	IMPACT	VIGILANTE	POTENCY
IDEALIST	NATURALIZATION	FREE SPACE	LIVID	POSTHUMOUS
SABOTEUR	VULNERABILITY	DREDGE	SEDATE	DISPERSING
ISSEI	RESCINDED	SPASM	PREMONITIONS	OBSTINANCE

Farewell to Manzanar Vocabulary

TURMOIL	INTANGIBLE	RESERVOIR	COLLABORATOR	GOUGING
VENTURE	PRECAUTIONS	AGITATING	PATRIARCH	CUBICLES
VIGIL	CRINGE	FREE SPACE	CAREENING	CAPITULATE
MAROONED	INTERNMENT	TROUGH	BARRACKS	PRIORITY
CONGESTION	ISSUE	FILIAL	EDICTS	SUSTENANCE

Farewell to Manzanar Vocabulary

ALIENS	POSTHUMOUS	CRINGE	ISSEI	AGITATING
VALIDATION	OVERT	SABOTEUR	OMINOUS	EDICTS
ASSIMILATE	IMPACT	FREE SPACE	VIGILANTE	VOLITION
PLACATOR	SANSEI	POTENCY	ACQUIESCENCE	CONFISCATORS
GROTESQUE	FLOURISH	AFFIRMED	ISSUE	SPASM

Farewell to Manzanar Vocabulary

IDEALIST	CHAOS	SUBDUED	TURBULENT	UNQUALIFIED
INTERNMENT	SEDATE	SURPLUS	VENTURE	PREMONITIONS
PRECAUTIONS	METAMORPHOSIS	FREE SPACE	CAREENING	GUILELESS
DISPERSING	OBELISK	CREDO	RESIGNED	CAPITULATE
COLLABORATOR	AUTHENTIC	PATRIARCH	NISEI	INEVITABLE

www.ingramcontent.com/pod-product-compliance
Lightning Source LLC
Chambersburg PA
CBHW081452070526
44586CB00019B/2322